Caring For Self
Caring For Others

Psychology and Spirituality for Daily Living

Robert J. Wicks, PsyD
Loyola College
Maryland

The Catholic Health Association
OF THE UNITED STATES

Library of Congress Cataloging-in-Publication Data

Wicks, Robert J.
    Caring for self—caring for others.

    Bibliography: p.
    A series of columns reprinted from the Catholic star herald, Camden, N.J.
    1. Spiritual life—Catholic authors. 2. Catholics—Mental health. I. Title. II. Catholic star herald. [DNLM: 1. Psychology—collected works. 2. Religion and Psychology—collected works. WM 7 W637c]
BX2350.2.W523   1987   248.4'82   87-11629
ISBN 0-87125-127-2

For My Patients

Contents

Acknowledgments

This book is primarily based on a series of articles I did for the *Catholic Star Herald* (Camden, NJ). To Jack Schibik, who encouraged me to write the column, and to Monsignor Charles Giglio, the executive editor, who continually encouraged me through his warmth and professionalism, I offer my deep appreciation. Also, I would like to express my appreciation and farewell to the Pastoral Counseling Department of Neumann College, especially my colleagues Rick Parsons and Joann Conn and my assistant Barbara Price, for providing a milieu where scholarship and service are deeply valued. In addition, I would like to note the support and enthusiastic spirit of Jacki Genello—she is truly a beautiful friend. Finally, and with the greatest sense of gratitude, I thank my wife Michaele for her editorial advice and personal generosity; her deep faith in God and our Christian friendship has made the road we take with our beautiful daughter Michaele, toward finding God each day a deeply rewarding journey.

RJW

Special Note To Readers

As in any book, especially one such as this, information is left out and topics are not covered; these should and can be included in future editions. If you do have a comment, question, or issue you would like covered in subsequent editions, I would enjoy hearing from you.

Dr. Robert J. Wicks
Pastoral Counseling Department
Loyola College Professional Center
7135 Minstrel Way
Columbia, Maryland 21045

Introduction

Small books are sometimes the best books. When we are in physical or emotional pain or see others who are dealing with such problems, we have a natural tendency to search for something and someone to lean on for support. At times such as these, reading a long volume may seem more trouble than it's worth. As an attempt to overcome this pitfall, the following book contains a group of brief essays that deal with common psychological and spiritual concerns. They are not meant to be read all at the same time, nor are they meant to replace longer, deeper works. Rather, they are designed to help us quickly recognize that our problems are not unique and that possible responses to what we are facing are not totally beyond reach. These essays emphasize that with prayer, reflection, and some sound information, the end of the dark tunnel can be seen. A ray of hope is possible.

Doubt, stress, illness, depression, turmoil, "burn out," confusion, failure . . . the list of troubles we and others face each day seems endless and occasionally overwhelming for all of us, even those of us who are in the role of "helper," "caregiver," or "minister." I hope the information that follows will not only provide initial help in dealing with these daily problems, but will also point to the need for trust in God and an openness to the Lord's presence when no solution that we find acceptable seems forthcoming.

Robert J. Wicks
Philadelphia
1987

Psychological Abortion
Of Adults

Einstein said: "He who can no longer pause to wonder and stand rapt in awe is as good as dead." This point is valid to no greater degree than in appreciating the loveliness of our uniqueness when we respond to the Spirit that is calling us to be.

A woman who had a miscarriage in the final trimester of her pregnancy taught me the importance of the uniqueness of every human being. When I asked her how she felt about losing her baby, she indicated that she was naturally quite sad about it, but there was one specific thing that particularly upset her:

"When I think of the son or daughter I lost, one point which tears me apart the most is that I shall never know who my child was . . . what he or she was like. Would he have been a hyperactive boy? Would she have been a pensive girl? I'll never know, and that is a special sadness for me."

We who do live, who have been born, and who have a personality that can be known by us and shared with others have a duty to let it evolve. If we don't seek to let the

1

Spirit grow within us but instead abort our talents, we mock existence and our singular place in it. In fact, the community (of saints) is significantly lessened by our absence.

Similarly, we must be aware of others in a way that is filled with awe and love. Just as we don't want to psychologically abort our own development, we also don't want to close our eyes to the growth of Christ in others.

The issue of abortion is a very serious one and one that is emphasized when we think of the right to life. Yet, as we have been taught in the doctrine of the "seamless garment," we must look at the threat to life in every aspect of society. That is why we cannot concentrate on fighting the abortion of children on one front and simultaneously ignore the destruction of our own and other adults' spirit to live and grow in Christ. To emphasize justice for the unborn while being too hard on ourselves or uncharitable to others is illogical. The psychological abortion of adults needs to be faced as well as the abortion of the unborn.

Therefore, we must see the challenge of charity as a priority. We must not "harden our hearts" and turn our backs on those who disagree with us, hurt us, are different from us, or those whom we fear. The beauty of the "Right to Life" movement is its call to all of us to love life right from the beginning. This beauty is tarnished when we become righteous or speak of religious principles with such venom that people see anger and hate instead of the love of God.

In practical terms we need to turn to others in a respectful way:
- Listen to your children; don't just preach to them. They have a right to be heard.
- Stop categorizing people into "good" and "bad" categories but look for the presence of God in everyone,

including (and maybe especially) those we view as manipulating, lazy, intrusive, too rigid, too liberal, too, too . . . well, too unlike we want them to be!

- Don't return anger with anger but instead with a question as to what they are angry about.
- Don't look at people with the question of what they can do for you but look at them as people to whom God gave a place on earth just like us.
- Don't look at others with all kinds of rules and expectations as to how they should behave if they are to receive attention from us. (It is all right to smile and say hello to people who don't have the freedom to say "hello" back. When this happens it doesn't mean we were stupid to greet them.)
- Ask yourself each day—not with a sense of guilt but with a real interest in learning how to improve—how have I been open to the people I have met today? How was I open to my friends, children, parents, colleagues, relatives, salespersons . . . everyone? If we ask this question enough we will be sensitive psychologically and spiritually to the community (of God) around us. We will be able to gather the little "crumbs" of emotional nourishment we gave in a smile to a neighbor, the few minutes we listened to our child or a co-worker, and the couple of minutes we chatted with a salesperson, and recognize that the "spiritual food" we gave out over the period of a day was enough to feed a multitude.

Let's end with a prayer: "Lord, may I pray and act to save the unborn and may I likewise open my heart to those who have been already granted the gift of birth and development. May I be kind to myself as you would so I may embrace your love, so I won't fear my mistakes in dealing with others but seek to learn from them. May I remember your greatest law: to love each other as you have and continue to love me. Amen."

Security and Simplicity

Sometimes we feel anxious almost from the moment we get up in the morning. At times like that we know we live in a troubled world because our world within reflects this fact. Our thoughts are going in forty different directions. There doesn't seem to be solutions to any of our problems. We wish we could get some closure on the issues, conflicts, and questions we have. We feel there are so many demands on our lives. We experience the loss of joy so many other people seem to have. We become nostalgic for the times in our lives when things were simpler, the times when we could laugh more easily. . . and the times we felt the gentle presence of God more naturally. . . the times when a child's smile or the presence of a crucifix or icon made us feel that God was with us and we were with him.

How can we recapture this sense of inner peace in a world so full of turmoil? How can we turn around and appreciate what we have and stop the insatiable march toward wanting more and more? How can we replace the tours of the mall designed to create a need for things that we didn't have before with a walk down the street, a trip to the museum or library, and a bowl of popcorn to carry us through watching an old movie? Maybe a return to simplicity can.

With simplicity we see the void in our lives. We recognize it as a sign that there is a God, that there is something greater than us, and that we can never fill this void without a spiritual relationship. We also don't try to fill the void with food, money, possessions, drugs/alcohol, friends, power, fame, or personal accomplishments. Life is certainly to be enjoyed, but it isn't designed to completely satisfy. To expect this is crazy, but aren't we all somewhat crazy in that each day we actually do fall into the error of expecting to be totally happy? The ironic part is that for those of us with some wealth, the problem is even greater at times because we forget that the only security we can have is the security that comes from depending on God. Rabbi Moshe Leib used to say: "How easy it is for a poor man to depend on God! And how hard it is for a rich man to depend on God. All his possessions call out to him: 'Depend on us!' " Anthony deMello echoes a similar theme in the following brief story:

"The disconsolate stockbroker lost a fortune and came to the monastery in search of inner peace. But he was too distraught to meditate. After he had gone, the Master had a single sentence by way of wry comment: 'Those who sleep on the floor never fall from their beds'."

To try to seek simplicity as a virtue doesn't mean for all of us that we must give away everything and live a life of radical poverty like St. Francis. However, it does mean that we must raise our consciousness to how we are being negatively influenced by the media, by some of our well-meaning colleagues, acquaintances, and friends, and by the themes and myths present in much of contemporary society. I think Richard Foster is onto something when he says in his book *Celebration of Discipline:* "The modern hero is the poor boy who become rich rather than the Franciscan or Buddhist ideal of the rich boy who voluntarily becomes poor. . . Covetousness we call ambition. Hoarding we call prudence. Greed we call industry."

Simplicity brings with it security. Simplicity encourages us to start each day and put our trust in God—not just in word but consciously, powerfully, and willfully in God. This means we say: "My security doesn't depend on what I own, who I know, how many people like me, and whether I succeed in doing all kinds of good things today (that preferably are noticed by a lot of people); my feelings of peace also are not destroyed by a loss of favor with others, a drop in the stock market, or the failure to get a good grade. My security only depends on one thing: an attention to the presence of God."

Simplicity also requires something. It requires us to stand before our lives and ask whether we need buy something that will put us in greater debt; it requires us to ask whether we are doing more and more because we worry about what other people think rather than what God wants; it requires us to stop trying to control life and safely manage the upcoming weeks, months, and years, so we can be open to enjoying today.

Simplicity takes the courage to let go of everything we have put so much faith in so we can enjoy all that is present to us. With a "spirituality of the now" it calls upon us to stop judging ourselves and others so we can have the energy to let others smile with us. If you are like me you already have too much. If you are like me you forget each day that even the ability to walk, or see, or hear, or breathe is a gift. Let's stop demanding and worrying so we can start enjoying life in a way that will also help others to smile and see God.

Steps To Nondefensive Communication

Defensiveness is such a waste of energy. It limits the joy of interpersonal relations, destroys initiative and creativity, and lowers a person's or group's morale. When these problems are compounded by the fact that defensiveness distorts communications and has a negative impact on personal, familial, work, and community relations, the seriousness with which we must take this problem is obvious. Therefore, the causes, signs, and methods of reducing defensiveness in communication are worth noting.

Causes of defensiveness in communication can be broken down into two categories: predisposing and precipitating. Predisposing conditions are low self-esteem and high sensitivity. The lower our self-esteem, the more we will be vulnerable to attacks or perceived attacks from others. If hypersensitivity is added to this, then the situation becomes more acute. In such an instance where this combination is present, a person's radar is up constantly and it seeks negative comments or circumstances in the environment that it can relate to the self to make it feel bad. Persons like this have a sensitivity to negativity that is analogous to fly paper—anything possibly negative in the

7

environment that can in any stretch of the imagination be personalized is in fact taken in and related to him/herself.

Precipitating factors that lead to defensiveness are quite varied. We must remember that in some cases it is natural to be defensive. If someone is personally attacking us rather than criticizing some aspect of our behavior, to react—possibly without reflecting on it first—is quite understandable.

However, other causes are common; they include: defensiveness on the part of the person we are interacting with; fear of rejection; exaggeration of a person's criticism; inappropriate expectations (expecting people to attack us or react negatively without anything on which to base this belief); feeling someone is questioning our abilities; and presenting a suggestion to someone at the wrong time (e.g., in front of others) or in an emotional/threatening way.

Defensiveness is fairly easy to observe from the outside. Yet, sometimes defensive people themselves are not as quick to observe it in their own behavior (e.g., I am not angry and defensive; I always shout when I feel you are prejudging me!) Some of the more obvious defensive reactions are: rigidity, attack, withdrawal, and camouflage. When we see someone who is unable to be open, keeps repeating their stand, and doesn't seem to have an understanding or empathy for another person's position —be it a good one or not—rigidity is evident. Attack, either in the form of an overt insult or the "long war" of passive-aggressiveness, is also another obvious sign of defensiveness. Withdrawal and camouflage may not be as obvious, however. Withdrawal can be guised in "niceness"; in such a case the person may seem to be listening and comprehending, but they are gripped in anxiety and are responding in a seemingly positive way because they fear further openness and intimacy. Camouflage, on the other hand, can involve either focusing on a detail or topic that will divert attention from the problem at hand or hiding behind a principle, rule, or detail so the bigger issue at hand can be kept at bay.

Defensiveness can be diffused and nondefensive communication techniques can be developed, however, if we keep several guidelines in mind trying to:

1. Increase our self-esteem by having a more accurate positive picture of ourselves. If we begin to assume we are all right as people, we will be less apt to be as sensitive or defensive even if other people are.

2. Deal with issues, not people. Stay away from name calling, and when someone does it to you, bring it to their attention and divert them back to the issues at hand.

3. Try not to predict failure in advance and catch yourself if you find yourself feeling defensive. The more you are open to the possibilities of an interaction and the more you lower your own defenses, the greater the chance for a nondefensive encounter.

4. Be specific, clear, and adult in your communication. By that I mean don't move all over the board or be vague or patronizing in communicating to others. Be to the point and honest in the way you are trying to bridge your understanding with the person with whom you are dealing. Once again, however, don't prejudge and precondemn the person but deal with the issues or misunderstanding in a way that makes handling the problem an exercise in learning.

If the above steps fail, sometimes a cooling off period is in order. Take time away from discussing it and come back to it later on when tempers are down and some space for sharing is present again.

9

All of this information won't solve all communications problems. And even good communication can't heal all; to think so is foolish. However, communication can set the stage for conversion, and in this light, anything we can do to encourage such a process should be undertaken.

Daily Lessons To
Improve Self-Esteem

I think all of us sometime in life try to resolve one or more basic personal conflicts:

- Having poor self-esteem
- Caring so much what other people think
- Hearing praise in a whisper and negative comments as thunder
- Being afraid of speaking up and saying what we really feel
- Being so very, very concerned about rejection

Such issues usually point out a self-esteem problem or a temporary lack of self-confidence. Given this, the overall issue becomes deciding how to deal with our problems in self-esteem.

To respond to this, we must first appreciate that the answer has both psychological and spiritual aspects. Psychologically, self-esteem issues originated early in life. The two primary sources are: the way we were treated and the problems in self-esteem that our parental figures had themselves.

11

No matter how much our parents—or the significant adults in our lives when we were young—liked us and tried to raise us correctly, there were many times when they gave us the impression that we were not enough as persons. To cite a little example, if we were clumsy and spilled something they might have said: "Watch what you are doing! You are so careless." In such an instance they focused on you rather than on your clumsy behavior. ("When we get excited we sometimes don't watch what we are doing and things get knocked over.") Since this is a fairly natural human behavior, we are exposed all through life to this kind of mini-attack on our person, so we begin questioning our self-esteem early in life. If you add to this the fact that we receive positive feedback when we do something good and disapproval when we fail in some way, you can begin to see that it is natural to have some sort of self-esteem issue in life. (Possibly that accounts for the saying: "Everyone is a bit neurotic.")

The other primary cause of self-esteem problems is our parent's own lack of security. In many ways without knowing it we pick up some of this lack of confidence and carry on the "family tradition" with respect to how secure we are in facing the world. Even in those instances where we are apparently more successful than our parents, underneath we often feel somewhat like charlatans.

Spiritually we follow suit with the psychological when we fail to trust completely that God loves us; that we are unique in God's eyes because we were created that way. Grace is a gift; and what we do—although important as a response to God's love—cannot earn us God's love. It is always there for us to enjoy.

So, given the above, what's the answer? How do we become self-confident and build up our self-esteem?

The first part of the answer is that there is no complete answer. In other words, to some extent we will never feel completely confident—after all, this is not paradise and anxiety will reign to some extent until the parousia (second coming of Christ). However, there are some simple, helpful steps we can take that will remove some of the unnecessary pain we feel in living life. We can ameliorate the condition by doing the following every day:

1. Imagery: image yourself as a special person; don't let the world tell you how you can become special through wearing certain clothes, having a particular job, enjoying many friends, or being well known. Instead, hold on—with all of your will and might—to the reality of John's Gospel, which indicates that Jesus called us his friends . . . his brothers and sisters.

2. Cognition: in your thinking pick up negative thoughts and timidity and answer them; tell yourself that you are thinking inappropriately negatively. In place put a realistic balancing positive thought.

3. Affect: when feeling low or insecure, look for the thought that is causing the feeling. Possibly you are personalizing something, exaggerating the negative, minimizing the positive, or making some type of cognitive distortion.

4. Behavior: act as if you are all right. This is not encouraging brashness or aggression; it is encouraging you to act based on a trust in God that you are all right as a person. It is encouraging you to act in a way that corresponds to how most people probably view you anyway—namely, that they find something special about you; they somehow see God in you and your presence to them.

Unconsciously, I think we are quite loyal to the negative. It is almost as if we learned a slightly negative view of ourselves long ago and hesitate to give it up. Even when we get positive feedback we somehow feel less and believe this feeling as if it were common sense or reality. Instead, such feelings are actually common nonsense. Maybe some of the things we do aren't good and need improvement, but we are always God's creation. If we trust in this, we will feel less insecure, be more able to do the will of God, and be more joyous and available to an anxious world that needs us.

The Elusive Route To Perspective

Several years ago I was talking with an anxious million-aire. He was deeply concerned about his financial status. He claimed that even though a million sounded like a lot, it wasn't really that much in comparison to others. Almost without thinking, I blurted out: "I wonder who your neighbors are?" He took this as a question to be answered and responded by listing the names of the chief executive officers of five of the Fortune 500 companies. My thought was: "I guess it is natural to think you're in need if you look out of his door, given the neighborhood he lives in."

In another session, I sat with a religious sister who was a very caring and committed person. She was constantly concerned about those in her local community and spent 60 hours each week in her apostolate. The topic of our conversation was her concern that she was letting people down and not being there enough for them. As I sat with her, I thought: "I wish you could see yourself in as posi-tive a light as I do. I wish you could appreciate how heal-ing your presence is to people, especially when you are not worried whether you are doing enough."

Perspective—it is so elusive, whether we are concerned about our material possessions, the service we do, or the view we have of ourselves. Since this is so, it is no wonder that so many people are depressed, anxious, or constantly competing with a goal that is never to be achieved. The almost compulsive search is for the "right" accomplishment, the "final" investment, the "truly understanding" friend, the "perfect" job, or the "ultimate" educational program. Unfortunately, the search is not being conducted in the right place; thus, it is never ending and continually frustrating.

With most of my patients, when this issue is raised, the question is asked: "Well where should I look?" (The implication is that I might actually know.) Since the question is a fair one, although the wrong one, my response is: "It is not so much where you look as it is when and how you look."

You first look when your mind first opens its eyes. As you lie in bed as soon as you begin to think, the thoughts should be turned toward God. Not in a pietistical way but in a manner that says something to the effect that: "During this day I shall remember you Lord, your love of me, and your love of others. These are not words I will take lightly or bother getting guilty over; these are words of the will that I shall take seriously and reflect on. If as you say, 'Those who do my will are my brothers and sisters', I shall try to do your will and learn from those instances where I fail."

This reflection continues later in the morning as we sit for 10, 15, or 20 minutes in quiet. We take this time to cement our commitment in prayer. And it continues during the day as we turn back to our promises by remembering them for 15 or 20 seconds. Then, as the day closes, we wrap ourselves in the warmth of God's acceptance and sit down and remember not only the day, which may have tired us, but the friendship we have with God amidst our failures and efforts. The "when" then is from the first dawn to nighttime in periodic doses. The "how" is in silence and gratitude.

This is not only a spiritual route to perspective, it is also a sound psychological one. When one of the past apostolic delegates to the United States was leaving his post to return to Rome, he cautioned the clergy and religious of the United States not to be merely social workers. In doing this, this brilliant Christian statesman did not imply that good works were not important. His main message, I think, was to let the works flow from your spiritual and theological presence. Otherwise you may lose your way. I think all of us—layperson, cleric, and religious alike—should reflect on this message of caution. Doing things and pasting God on our lives as an afterthought is a sure way to lose perspective. And taking time out to reflect and pray is a sure way to retain perspective . . . even amidst pain, confusion, and stress.

New Beginnings
Through Spiritual Reflection

A funny thing happens to most of us every fall. Even if we are not in school, don't work in school, don't have children in school, or have not been in school for a long time, we seem to experience September as the beginning of a new year. So, although January 1st gets the credit, the real new beginnings seem to belong to the first week in September.

It's as though from our many years in school we have imprinted in our psyche the academic calendar. Even nature can't convince us otherwise. After all, what happens in the fall? Leaves die, most of nature goes to sleep, and most of the green that has cooled us off disappears. Nature tells us it is a new ending. However, Sister told us years ago it was a new beginning. Who are you going to believe? Right—nature doesn't have a chance; we'll go with what Sister told us every time!

So if we are to make new resolutions and seek new ways to see God and let God be seen in us (i.e., our behaviors, attitudes, and visions), maybe fall is the time to do it. Maybe fall is the time to both throw a party and get on our knees; maybe fall is a time to have renewed hope and a new journey in faith; maybe fall is a time to risk being Christian by seeing what exciting ways Christ is calling us to dump our domesticated faith and find the Spirit of Peace in a different way.

But how do we do this? We've tried to do it in the past and it hasn't worked very well. (Last January's resolutions fell apart before February had a chance to attempt to depress us.) Well, maybe we shouldn't try to change. Instead, maybe this time—possibly for the first time—we should simply try to face reality and listen to God. And when we do that change will happen without our efforts; after all, doesn't holiness come to all who are open to grace? That's what I thought anyway.

So, how can we face reality and listen to God? Well, I suggest the simple approach. It's probably so simple you may already be doing it, so all you need do is continue; the only change being that you do it with greater interest and—more important—with greater love. Also, I suggest even if you feel you already do what I am about to suggest that you check yourself to see if you really do. (People who are in need of a "diet" from food, cigarettes, liquor, sleep, work, or some other "idol" will often say they don't eat, drink, etc., much.)

What I suggest is that you read a little of the Bible in the morning (maybe the day's readings from the Missal), stay quiet for fifteen minutes, and do that five or six days a week. I also encourage thinking about what you have been thinking and feeling during the day; a good time to do this is early in the afternoon. (Do this in a way that helps you learn about yourself—not blame yourself or someone else for problems.)

Stay quiet at night for about five minutes; take out an icon or a picture (a field, a stream, a home . . .) that you

19

can look at in love and appreciation for life, for God (if you close your eyes during this quiet period and it helps, fine; however, many people start thinking about a million things when they close their eyes after a full day). And finally, read one spiritual book this fall and winter. That's right—one. Your schedule is probably so full that any more than that would be nice but impossible. Read one book as if it were the last and only book on earth. Read it in earnest, read it with love, and try to ask yourself: "What is God asking of me in this book?" If in doing this, you become guilty, it is not God speaking to you. Guilt is not going to help you focus on your blocks or help you learn; it's only going to make you feel bad. And isn't it silly for you in your pursuit of God to feel bad? Feeling bad will only make you give up the whole thing.

Instead, your pursuit should inspire you to ask questions as: How can I make my life more simple? How can I share my love and stop trying to fill the void that can only be filled by God (i.e., through more and more possessions, trips, food, excitement . . .)? How can I learn to laugh more? How can I trust I am all right as a person so I can let down my defenses and my desire to control everyone and just be me, so people can be attracted to me because they see God in me and they see God's reflection in themselves?

Life really is simple. We make it complex and harder when we try to find justice and try to be secure in it through our own efforts. We appreciate its simplicity, on the other hand, when we seek God and love ourselves and those around us in a new way. Good luck on your new beginnings . . . and pray for me; I'm beginning again, too!

Being "Out Of Sorts"

At a certain time each month, for about three or four days, we may feel swamped by negative feelings. We feel both sad and angry, and all the hurts, rejections, and disappointments in life seem to face us. When it's happening, we are very sensitive and say things that are out of character. However, when it's over we think, "Oh, it's just something physical"—"that time of the month," and try to forget it. Yet, the vague feeling still remains: "Is there something I can do about this so I'm not constantly faced with this pattern or must I just grit my teeth and bear it until it passes given its possible hormonal cause?"

There are times in the day, month, or year that, because of physiological reasons, we are more apt to become hypersensitive to negative memories and the way people are treating us. Lack of sleep, daily stress, insufficient nutrition, inadequate exercise (which involves the necessary oxygen-carbon dioxide exchange), and hormonal changes all can account for temporary periods in which the unpleasant past and the way people treat us in the present can become heightened in our sense of awareness. Certainly the period prior to menses is one of those times, especially for those persons subject to particularly dramatic hormonal shifts in their bodies.

During these times, our perception of the present and our recall of the past tend to be distorted. We tend to see things through a negative filter, which then leads us to create patterns from experiences in our life that are not accurate. When this occurs, we seem caught. If we ignore what we are going through, we tend to become overwhelmed almost without our knowing it. This can lead to unexpected sarcasm or large outbursts on our part. On the other hand, if we try to look at our feelings and thoughts, the situation doesn't seem much better: we either wind up condemning ourselves or indicting others. Thus, when for some physiological reason we get tossed around, we feel lost; when it passes, the temptation is just to give thanks and say, "Oh, I was just tired." Or, "It was my period; I'll just forget the whole thing." However, the only problem with this is that this time in our life goes by each time without any benefit to us. There is another alternative.

During those times when hypersensitivity to others, sarcastic remarks, and "negative remembering" occur, there are a number of steps we can take to control and learn from the situation. These steps include: recognition, silence, note-taking, and reflection. The first step, *recognition*, is quite helpful because it alerts us to the fact that we seem overly sensitive to how we are interpreting others' comments and actions. If we can pick up those times when we seem more vulnerable to the normal rough spots in life and the periods when we are more apt to look back at life's past hurts, we have made the first major step in dealing with physiologically induced valleys in our life.

The second step, *silence*, is helpful so we don't do something based on inaccurate perception. When I feel tired or for some reason "testy," I try to maintain as low a profile as possible. Silently I try to listen to my environment and see how I am interpreting it and the kinds of things from my past that I am recalling.

The third step, which is based on what I have picked up during my "silent listening," is *note-taking*, or writing in a journal, stemming from what I thought and felt during the day. This then leads to the fourth step, which is the key to the process: *reflection*. However, this reflection is not done while I am still feeling low. I put the notes aside until I am thinking more accurately and positively. It is at that point I look at them to see what negative feelings are lurking underneath.

Such unhealed memories and unfinished business in life should be evaluated so we can deal with them and let go of them. As Henri Nouwen notes in his book *The Living Reminder*, if we continue to repress such memories and feelings about how we were treated in life, they will continue to have a force in our life, albeit an unconscious one.

The goal then when we are thrown up and down in life for physiological reasons is to recognize when this happens, silently note what poignant feelings and thoughts come up, and learn from these negative forces by looking at them reflectfully and prayerfully *after* the period passes. All we can do during the time is to constantly tell ourselves our distortion is *temporarily* negative and this feeling will pass.

Relationships

"Openness" and a healthy, clear appreciation of your own personality are probably two of the most essential building blocks in the formation and growth of relationships. Relationships are beneficial when they are open and free. The more conditioned they need to be, the less healthy and mature they are. The limits we place on others, and the ones we feel we must respond to from others, are often really unnecessary and destructive. There is a temptation to fool ourselves into believing that certain conditions are merely understandable expectations. Yet, in our hearts we can recognize the fallacy of this by the negative feelings and tensions they engender. Any relationship that can't be trusted is not worth having.

Henri Nouwen, during his Genessee experience, came to this in his appreciation of how easy it is to limit and distort even the most beautiful interpersonal experience open to us, the one we call "love." He said, "It is important for me to realize how limited, imperfect, and weak my understanding of love has been . . . .My idea of love proves to be exclusive: 'You only love me truly if you love others less'; possessive: 'If you really love me, I want you to pay special attention to me'; and manipulative: 'When you love me, you will do extra things for me'. Well, this idea of love easily leads to vanity: 'You must see something very special in me'; to jealousy: 'Why are you now suddenly so interested in someone else and not in me?' and to anger: 'I am going to let you know that you have let me down and rejected me'."

Opening up a place in our heart for others so we might be available to them, and in turn be gracious enough to appreciate the warmth of their gifts of self, is a difficult mystery of living. Because as people we tend to be so needy, there are so many nuances of openness that can be violated without our even knowing it. In the words of Thomas Hora, "To be interested is to love and revere; to be inquisitive, however, is to intrude, trespass, violate." However, to have healthy relationships with others, we must be clear about our relationship with ourself. The relationship with self determines how we deal with the world and how we view ourselves.

View of self and the world at large is unique to each person. No matter how much someone likes or hates us, knows or is unfamiliar with us, no one will ever view us or the world quite the same way we do. The reason for this is that we are unique. In psychological terms, we each have a singular feature called "the personality."

So to understand our relationships with others, there must first be an appreciation of how we relate to ourselves. If we are relaxed with ourselves, we will be at ease with others. If we feel insecure in terms of our own self-esteem, we will constantly be comparing ourselves to others. Relationship with self goes hand in hand with a relationship with others. As Pope John XXIII noted, "Whoever has a heart full of love always has something to give."

Learning To Give and
Receive Love

Probably the biggest problem I encounter in my therapy practice is the inability to give and receive love. Many people who come to me are unable to experience love when it is present or give it without a lot of strings attached.

Many of us have had difficult experiences in childhood or are undergoing them now. Feeling the love of others and sharing of ourselves is quite difficult then. However, the only answer is to open our eyes to the love that is in the world, our world, and to give with a spirit of *mitzvah* (to give without expecting anything in return.)

As I write this, I am thinking of a person I meet about once a week. When we meet I smile and ask, "How are you doing?" She usually complains that no one appreciates her, she doesn't get a chance to be what she is able to be, and generally she has a depressed look on her face. Each time I leave her I wonder if she presents such a negative picture to each person she meets and wonder if that is part of the reason people avoid her or treat her negatively. Also, I wonder—doubt actually—whether when

26

she meets me during her day she is a bit happier having experienced my smile and interest in her. My heart tells me "I hope so" but my head says, "My smile probably rolled off her back, whereas anything that she probably could interpret as negative stuck like glue." However, anytime I am tempted to give up on her and join others who probably have, I remember a story told by Mother Teresa:

"We have a place in Australia. When we went around in that place, we found an old man in a most terrible condition. I went in there and tried to talk to him and then I said to him, "Kindly allow me to clean your place and clean your bed and so on." He answered, "I'm all right!" I said to him, "You will be more all right if I clean your place." In the end he allowed me to do it and when I was in his room I noticed that he had a lamp, a very beautiful lamp but covered with dirt and dust. I said to him, "Do you not light the lamp?" And he said "For whom? Nobody comes here. I never see anybody. Nobody comes to me. I don't need to light the lamp." Then I asked him, "If the sisters come to you, will you light the lamp for them?" He answered, "Yes, I'd do it!" So the sisters started going to him in the evening and he used to light the lamp. Afterwards (he lived for more than two years), he sent word to me through the sisters and said, "Tell my friend, the light she lit in my life is still burning!"

As lovers we must persevere. We must have low expectations and high hopes. We must also be open to love wherever and whenever we experience it. William Johnston, SJ, says in his beautiful and profound book, *Christian Mysticism Today*, " . . . the great challenge of the Christian life is to receive love, to open our hearts to the one who knocks, to accept him into the very depths of our being . . . authentic human love is God's love made incarnate. So accept the love which comes your way. If you think that nobody loves you, this is probably because you are unconsciously warding off love. You are just not taking it in. Accept it with gratitude and you will experience joy."

The problem of loneliness and feeling a lack of love is a serious and common one in the United States. Mother Teresa sees it as a deeper poverty than currently being experienced in Ethiopia and Calcutta. "To the hungry there, you give them bread and their eyes light up in love and gratitude; to people here where bread is plentiful, the hunger for love is the problem we face."

So, what is the answer? Well, naturally I don't know the answer. However, I do have my response, and it isn't very original for it follows the one given by Jesus and the two people quoted here: accept love wherever and whenever it is given, and give it with a sense of *mitzvah*. We must try to share love from the innermost circle outward.

In other words, we must love the Lord by loving his presence within us—we must love and respect ourselves. Then, we must love our family and those we meet each day, even if they are grouches. Then, we must love those in each part of our city, state, and wherever, rather than concentrating on whether they are getting more out of life than we are. (Naturally, this is a tall order, but we have the rest of our life to strive to fulfill it.) Finally, we must seek to embrace the smiles, good words, and friendship others give us, not desperately and by trying to hold onto and smother the person who shares with us, but gently and respectfully. In William Johnston's words once again, "Accepting love, we (need to) return it not only to God but to people—to everyone we meet without exception."

Appreciate the "Now"
In the Rush To the Future

We seem to lament the passage of time. Most of us have said in a wistful voice at one time or another: "Time passes too quickly." Often we seem to be wishing we had more time, more space, more opportunity to enjoy the moments of life. And, for those moments when some thing special did occur, we have photo album reminders.

However, alongside of this attitude seems to be another diametrically opposed one that gives rise to the way we face each day. It is a future-oriented vision that never seems to let us explore the "now" to see what it might have in store for us.

Parents can be heard saying: "I can't wait until she's in school, beyond adolescence, graduated from college, has a good job (as is evidenced by a never ending string of promotions), is married, has children . . ." Most who work seek to somehow sweep away the week and exclaim in a voice of accomplishment: "Thank goodness it's Friday!" Given the presence of this attitude then and the lament about how time is flying, I think the real question we must face in life is: "Why am I rushing through the 'now'?"

Where are we going in such a hurry? Why is it that we are so willing to give up the opportunity to appreciate today . . . each day? If we are on a moving train going from Philadelphia to New York, we don't rush from the back of the train to the front so we can get to our destination more quickly; that would be ridiculous. Yet, we seem constantly to be in motion trying to get to the special times of the day, week, month, or year.

We even do this in life. We look to the time when we can be this, do this, or be secure and happy. We act as if the present is devoid of reward and the future is a guaranteed time of plenty. The only result is we miss so much and we look forward to things to such a degree that when we get there we don't even know how to enjoy them—instead we look yet ahead to further so-called rewards or feel frustrated that we can't enjoy what we've worked for and yearned for so long.

Each day as I drive to work, and the same attitude tries to overtake me, I look at a beautiful house that a man built for himself over a period of two years. He was so excited about the prospect of living there, and I can understand why. It is a very nice house. The only problem is that just after he moved in, he died.

Each day is the only day we have. Each day, no matter how tedious our job, how many diapers our youngest goes through, how busy our schedule, there are opportunities for us to *see* . . . to *respond* . . . to *appreciate*.

How we do it doesn't take a special talent or an inordinate amount of training; all it takes is persistence and attention to the ordinary and the incidental. Henri Nouwen used to tell the story of the man who said: "My whole life I was complaining about interruptions to my work until I discovered my interruptions were my work." In line with this, I try to appreciate the "now" by paying as full attention as I can to the person I'm with. (I don't always do so well, but the trying helps me to be more present than if I didn't try.) Another approach is to see people where they are now—at this age, at this point in time—as "gift." So, if my teenager is a pain, I try to appreciate what she's going through, get involved in this whole time of her life, laugh at myself as I try to reason with her and usually fail ("success" naturally would be if she listened to every wonderful word of wisdom I give her), and try to appreciate our struggling relationship.

What's the alternative? Probably to run through life saying: "Where did her growing up years go? . . . Boy, time flies, doesn't it?"

Endless Activity...Step Back and Be Silent

We are surrounded by so much stimuli: things to do, books to read, people to see, activities in which to be involved, prayers to be said, good works to be done . . . the list is literally endless! In response to this we will try almost anything to keep things under control; so, we make a list of things to do and in the process have another thing hanging over our heads—a list.

In response to all of this, we feel we must do something or all will be lost. The real response I think is not to do something but to step back, be silent, and try to recognize our temptation to avoid silence by involving ourselves in the widely reinforced process of compulsive activity. If we can recognize some of the reasons for avoiding silence and can appreciate the lure of doing, doing, doing, then maybe we can transform our attitude about life and have the courage to set priorities better. James Whitehead, for instance, wrote in an article on "An Asceticism of Time" that "Christian time management, as an asceticism, will always be understood as a response to grace, to the invitation to become less scattered and more aware of the Present already there . . .

Distress often arises not from doing bad, nor failing to act, but, intriguingly, from doing too much good."

Brother David Steindl-Rast supports this point in his recently widely read book, *Gratefulness*, when he says: "We may have to learn that the useless deserves prime time. The superfluous comes first in the order of importance. The necessary will claim our attention anyway. To acknowledge this truth might mean a far more drastic transformation by divine glory than we were prepared to undergo. It might turn our set of values topsy-turvy. When Jesus says, 'Behold the lilies' (Mt 6:28), he is inviting each one of us to take beauty seriously in all its uselessness. What will this mean for our daily life? . . . The do-gooder is too busy. He has no time to bother with flowers . . . the busybody does not understand the language of . . . (the lilies') silent eloquence. He rushes on: 'Sorry, I don't speak Lily.' His ears are buzzing with the din of his own projects, ideas, and good intentions."

Compulsive activity also has the "advantage" of helping us to avoid silence. Even those of us who always claim that we resent not having enough free time and quiet periods may be included in this group. William Johnston notes in his recent book on mysticism that "when one's senses are no longer bombarded by all the junk to which we are ordinarily exposed, when the top layers of our psyche are swept clean and bare and empty—then the deeper layers of the psyche rise to the surface. The inner demons lift up their ugly faces." Parker Palmer puts this less dramatically but just as forcefully when he says: "I had come to the silence with a headful of religious ideas and beliefs. In the silence, they all fell away, structures without foundations. In the silence I was forced to confront the ambiguities of my own religious experience, and

I grew angry about what I found there, about the discrepancies between my inherited faith and my own faithless life."

So, in addressing our overactivity, we must be willing to risk facing ourselves in silence and facing others who have expectations of us that include doing much and always being available. This isn't easy, but as almost everyone recognizes, the alternatives—unbridled activity and undisciplined activism—lead only to an exhaustion of both mind and heart. And so, when we are caught in a swirl of activity, it is a signal to us to seek God in it . . . to quiet down and let the depth of the quiet silently challenge us to form our days in a way that we don't run through them.

Let me quote a brief paragraph in a little work I did on the topic of availability: "Availability is a great gift; it is a gift to behold, a gift to cherish, a gift to share. Yet, as in any living gift, availability must be nurtured if it is to thrive and be a continual source of joy. The challenge is knowing how and when to do this; and the satisfaction is in knowing that if we continually try to be open to God, we will never lose it."

New Year...Old Gifts

Special things sometimes get lost or are taken for granted. And, in the process, they lose the unique quality they originally held for us. A while back columnist Darrell Sifford interviewed me about this in the *Philadelphia Inquirer.* When I made my "confession" about how I kept things new and vital, my neighbors and friends teased me about it for months. I told them that I often tried to renew "psychological snapshots" in my life; I did things to remember the excitement and wonder of certain experiences surrounding people and things that are still part of my life today.

In the case of the house I now live in, I remember the first time I walked into it and the excitement it held for me. I was a perennial apartment dweller and the house actually had a fireplace and a garbage disposal! (However, I must confess that after buying the house, I discovered that the garbage disposal had no blade.) What I mentioned in that interview several years ago with respect to this is that at times I stand across from my house and walk into it and try to reimagine what it was like on the snowy day I originally stepped into it.

You see, if I don't do this, somehow I take the house for granted. I forget how lucky I am. That's easy to do because my acquaintances and friends often have houses that are "better" or more unique. Unconsciously, when they visit they might even put the house down or go on and on as to how I might improve it so it can be special. Also, the houses in the neighborhood are as nice and it is easy to say "So what" about the place I live in now. But at these times I try to recall the excitement I felt on my first visit and the expression of awe on my mother's face when she saw the house during her first visit on a Thanksgiving Day.

The advertising media would always have us believe that we need more, something additional, something new. When actually what we really need to do is dust off, rewrap, and open anew something we already have. Maybe that is the value of international travel and one of the benefits that those of us who were in the armed forces have had. We can more readily get in touch with how much we already have.

In my circle of friends and probably in yours, one of the seemingly national pastimes is to focus on what you don't have or have lost. "This friend and I no longer speak to each other." "The stock market has gone down, or I just missed investing in something good and look at how well it has done." "I used to be able to do so much more but now I can't." "The church used to be _____ and now it's not."

The list of our lacks and losses is endless. The problem: we have lost perspective; we have lost the reality that all is gift. While we focus on the injustice in our lives, we fail to open our hearts and accept the love and many, many gifts that sit undusted, unappreciated, and unused right at our side . . . or right in our families, places of work, congregations, and parishes.

Sometimes it takes a death, a loss, a crisis, or a traumatic awakening to blow the dust away. But it needn't take such an event. We can do it slowly each day, because the dust of taking things and people for granted naturally builds up each day. The question is: Will we take out time each morning, each day, each evening to look . . . to look anew, so that all that is gift is embraced instead of being given away through neglect and lack of appreciation? Possibly this is the question to reflect on every new year as our resolutions are shaped and placed in our hearts.

Ten Ways To Beat the Post-Holiday Blahs

Down periods are natural after holidays such as Christmas, but they can be transformed into a very special time of the year if we are willing to take several steps with regard to our attitude (thinking) and behavior.

Enjoy the quiet time. During the holidays we rush around shopping, going to parties, and preparing for Christmas. Then, in a blink it's over, the tree is down and the Christmas carols are silent for another year. However, what we often fail to remember is that as Christians the Christmas season is not over for us. It has just begun! Therefore, we can celebrate it in a thoughtful, relaxing way more in line with the real message of Christmas than the one that the media tries to sell us. In the cold, quiet January and February evenings and weekends we can:

- *Spend more time with the family.* During the holidays it is such a rush we rarely have time to converse or recreate at home with those we love.

- *Read.* Too often we get lost in the TV and move through the evening like a robot. You can still watch TV but take out at least one-half hour to read.

- *Write a letter.* This is a lost art because of the wide-spread use of the telephone now. However, we can and do say things in letters that we can't say over the phone. If you feel you are not a letter-writer, become one. On a scrap of paper outline ten things you would say to this person if he/she were in your presence, then write a paragraph for each point. (If you have no one to write to, then write a letter to your local newspaper about something you feel strongly.)

- *Build a relationship with God.* You have talked about prayer, read about prayer, and complained you don't have time to pray. Now you do . . . so pray. Just take out about 15 to 30 minutes a day (preferably at the same time) and read a few verses of the Gospel/Epistles and just sit in silence and let them nurture you. Or, just read something spiritual (any book by Henri Nouwen, Thomas Merton, Anthony Bloom, or David Steindl-Rast should do if you can't find someone you particularly like), and reflect on what they are trying to tell you about God.

Celebrate in a different way. We are so used to celebrating in the way we're taught in society (e.g., big parties) that we forget celebration need not involve a lot of noise and liquor or drugs. Other ways we can celebrate are:

- *Take a Saturday morning family outing.* You can combine a Saturday morning mass with a trip out for breakfast.

- *Bundle up and go outdoors.* We are so mall-oriented that we fail to get the positive results of a short walk outside, a trip to a sports event, a walk in the town closest to us, or a train ride to a local city or a visit to friends/family missed during the holidays.

- *Invite friends over.* Although you may be "partied-out," a quiet evening with friends can be a relaxing community exercise that doesn't have to cost a lot of money or be very hectic. Lower your expectations and desire to impress others, get some cheese and summer sausage, and invite someone over for a couple of hours to chat, watch a TV special with you, or play some Scrabble. It need not be a big deal.

- *Volunteer your services.* You may feel, "How is that going to help?" Or, "How is that celebrating?" When we reach out to someone else (and there are plenty of opportunities to help out at the local parish, school, hospital, or community organization), it helps us to stop focusing negatively on ourselves. It is also a way of celebrating our gifts, good fortune, and faith in a way that leaves us with a sense of peace instead of a hangover.

The above are just some ideas. Try them or add your own, but the key is not to be inordinately pulled down by short periods of the blahs. Enjoy this quiet time of year and seek to break things up with different kinds of mini-celebrations.

Dealing With
"Chronic Niceness"

Anger is a human emotion that is neither good nor bad; it just is. Like alcohol, it is not evil in itself, and just like alcohol it can be abused. Whereas most of us realize that it is wrong to impulsively vent our anger against others, as Christians many of us are not aware of problems at the other end of the spectrum: namely, avoiding the recognition and presence of anger at all costs so as to appear loving and accepting of everyone under all circumstances . . . "chronic niceness."

Worshipers and people in ministry, and the social setting in which they operate (i.e., church, religious community, Christian school), often consciously support a style of behavior emphasizing control, suppression, denial of anger, and avoidance of conflict. As one might expect, such a psychological philosophy of living can easily lead to personal devastation, apathy, or supposed religious causes that are based on legalism or extremism and unconsciously deliver hostility instead of the Good News of the Gospel. Illustrations of this, unfortunately, are easy to uncover. The following are four obvious ones:

41

- The "nice"—but insular and stagnant—Christian church or school that is so fearful of anger being experienced in its midst that it discourages and denies conflict in any form

- The accommodating priest or lay leader who gets along with everyone in the parish but develops an ulcer, hypertension, and/or problems with alcoholism or obesity in the process

- The religious worker who does everything by the letter of the law and devotes much energy to keeping himself or herself from breaking it and to ensuring that others don't venture out of its bounds as well

- The Christian activists (e.g., for peace) who act with such a vengeance that their message defeats the purported Christian one they claim to be delivering to others by witnessing the truth.

Such examples of Christians who are not in touch with their anger, much less aware of their ability and need to use it constructively, can be traced to the traditional misunderstandings that Christians have with regard to anger.

Once we as Christians stop seeing the emotion of anger as being either good or bad and recognize it as a sign of personal vitality, we will be able to distinguish between *experiencing* anger on the one hand and expressing or dealing with it on the other. Christian assertiveness avoids both "swallowing" or denying anger and the opposite extreme of confusing assertiveness with aggression and believing that we should fight back by stamping on others first or in return.

Christian assertiveness is grounded in a belief that we as effective persons can and should *recognize* and *understand* what makes us angry; be able to relate the feelings of anger we have to a specific issue; find the courage to *own* our anger by asking the question, "How did I make myself so angry?" rather than "How did he make me angry?"; and be able to communicate our concerns to others in a manner that does not unduly raise defensiveness.

It is also based on an appreciation of the fact that sometimes we are angry with others because our needs or expectations are unrealistic. When they are realistic, Christian assertiveness calls for an openness that does not justify being aggressive and driving others away, that does not glorify passivity and prevent a free, real interchange, but allows angers to be dealt with as they arise rather than when they blow up after a long period of being buried in a sea of "niceness."

The owning of anger is essential not only to promote honest interpersonal relations among us as Christians but also to help us focus clearly on the validity of being angry at injustices and disgusted with what is wrong with society today. Anger is not only a personal human emotion but also at times a sign of our intense concern for others. It alerts us to the frustration of our realistic and unrealistic needs, and it also points out when others are touching sensitive areas in our psychological makeup or are committing community injustices that are personally unacceptable. Anger, then, can be a diagnostic tool to help us learn about ourselves, our defenses, our limits, and our beliefs, but such diagnosis cannot take place if anger is seen as forbidding and is buried before it can be utilized for what it is.

Therefore, we should be sensitive each day to when and how we make ourselves angry. When we feel our "buttons" being pushed by something or someone, we then need to ask ourselves, "Why?" Following this, we need to put the issue in specific, neutral terms and bring it up with the goal of trying to find a solution to it. And, if our effort to communicate and deal with the problem doesn't work, we should take care not to castigate ourselves or the person(s) at whom we are angry; let us remember that patience is also a virtue. (For additional reading on this: David Augsburger: *Anger & Assertiveness in Pastoral Care*, Fortress Press.)

No Strings Attached: The True Spirit Of Helping

Being a sensitive helper isn't easy. Recently, a woman who often helped others reported that she thought most people appreciated her assistance. However, she also noted that in some instances others seemed to take advantage of her, were sarcastic, or seemed to vent their anger on her. She was very sensitive, so when that happened she felt terrible and wondered if she was too good to people. So she would withdraw for a while and then would start the whole process all over again. Others would tell her to "toughen her skin" but she didn't feel right being callous or rude to people.

Sensitive people such as this woman are beautiful. Caring is necessary. . . especially in a world so intent on personal survival and narcissism. So the question in my mind is: "How can we preserve the sensitive caring person so her love can continue and no undue pain is taken on by her?"

Neil Richardson once noted that: "Jesus taught that God was not only more demanding than people cared to think, but also more generous than they dared to hope." In helping others we need to respond to both the Lord's demand and his generosity. In responding to the call to reach out to others in need, we have to face the reality that hurt people hurt others—including those who wish to help them.

A few common examples:

- The adolescent who is in the midst of the turmoil of physical and emotional changes he is going through who is disrespectful to parents and teachers because he is so confused inside
- The single parent who vents her anger against the director of religious education because of the diocesan guidelines she must follow if her child is to be confirmed
- The frustrated co-workers in need of a vacation or a break from the tough year that has just past who are starting to get on each others' nerves

The list is endless.

In such instances when we reach out, people will respond often in a negative fashion. Sometimes we are surprised by this; we feel if we assure others and help them, they will do the same for us. We turn the other cheek and expect that they will be overwhelmed by our goodness. Instead, psychologically they hit us right in the face.

When this happens, we should not take it to heart. Often their reaction—or the extent of it—is not directed at us. On the other hand, we shouldn't ignore it— because letting them be angry and hostile without bringing it to their attention doesn't help either. So, in such a case we might say: "You seem angry. Are you angry at me or someone or something else?"

If we are troubled that people are not appreciating us or are taking us for granted, this is a sign that we are either not setting limits for them or our expectations are unrealistic. People will often ask for unrealistic attention or help, if we give them the signal that we won't say "no." Also, sometimes we forget that we help not so others will appreciate that we are wonderful people but because we want to share Christ with them . . . to be holy. As Kenneth Leech notes in his book *True Prayer:* "Holiness manifests the character, the nature of God . . . . Holiness never points to itself but always beyond itself to God. The saint is essentially someone who communicates and radiates the character of God, his love, his joy, his peace . . . . And the world needs saints, Simone Weil wrote, just as a plague-stricken city needs doctors."

To gain perspective and continue helping amidst the turmoil in a world filled with stress and bent on destruction because it believes it can fight hate with aggression, the answer is love: to both give it and receive it. To be attuned to it, we must both be willing to receive it from others in the way they smile, the way they struggle, the way they try to live in a tough world. When you see someone who doesn't appreciate your efforts or who has a temper, don't take it to heart but remember that somewhere in their broken heart is God. Maybe you are not the one chosen to reach them and that is all right, but don't fall into the danger of disliking yourself or the other person if you don't feel like your helping is making a difference. Sometimes only God knows when and how we make a difference.

Finally, and most importantly, during these times when we feel we are getting nowhere and no one seems to appreciate our efforts, we need to move closer and closer to God in prayer. As Teresa of Avila says: "He never tires of giving . . . let us never tire of receiving." If you feel just as terrible in prayer as in life, don't worry—instead just stay there feeling terrible . . . and your patience will be rewarded. For, instead of feeling unloved, unappreciated, and unaccepted for what you do and who you are, you will soon feel a peace amidst the turmoil, and it is in the field of peace that real joy— the Joy of the Spirit—grows best.

Holiness Adds Peace,
Not Pressure, To Your Life

Persons who are referred to as the "middle class" often report that they feel "fed up" with everything. The following statements give a flavor of this feeling: "I'm over-taxed, overworked, and overburdened. The harder I work, the less I seem to get ahead. Then, when I go to church on Sunday and hear a sermon encouraging me to help the poor and be holy, I wonder how much more I can do, and what else the Church or God expects of me. At the end of a hard work day, I often can't help feeling resentful."

Many, if not most, of the middle class have worked very, very hard to get to this position in life, and they are holding onto it by a thread. If they hear the Church on Sunday calling them to take on even more tasks in life—a life that is already filled to the brim—their anxiety is understandable.

However, I'm not sure if that is exactly what the Church is calling us to do today—namely, merely to take on additional tasks in the name of Christ. I think instead, in the sermons, writings, and parish groups that accurately

49

reflect God's call to us, the message is to "be holy, because I, the Lord your God, am holy" (Lev. 19:1-4). The implications of this are very important for middle-class persons.

If we hear the Church's message as a guilt trip designed to merely make us work more, for some reason the wrong thing has been communicated to us. The natural response to this is to be resentful or do a few or many things until you are tired. On the other hand, the Church—the institutional and, in the broader sense of the term, the "people of God"—is supposed to help create a milieu in which holiness is seen as something possible and desirable.

By holiness, I don't mean the pietistical notion of hands folded, smiling serenely, and looking like a poorly done plaster statue. When I speak of holiness, I mean an angle of vision, a perspective, a way of viewing, thinking, and acting in the world. In the words of James Fenhagen, the Dean of General Theological Seminary in New York City, "Holiness . . . is a political word. A holy person is a person who sees the world, if only momentarily, through the eyes of Christ and is drawn to act in response to this vision."

Today in this troubled world where we are all under so much pressure, the call to holiness is not so much a call to add to our pressures but is rather a call to view the world in a different way amidst the pressures. Paradoxically, the call to be holy, instead of adding things to our schedule, can actually transform it in a way where we feel more peace.

People I know who are under a great deal of pressure, and who deal with many troubled people and difficult situations that would try the patience of a saint, maintain their sense of balance by taking several simple steps to maintain perspective. These steps don't add much to the day in terms of tasks or chores to do but the result is that they help to transform their attitudes. The steps are as follows:

1. They start their day with about 15 to 20 minutes (or more) in prayer and reflection. They read the daily readings from Scripture or some spiritual reading and then sit quietly with it.

2. During the day they take out a few minutes to reflect on how the day is going and how they have responded to it. They don't do this to blame themselves for their faults, but to learn from the experiences they have had. Essentially, they pose the question, "What if I were to die now; would today's thoughts, actions, and feelings on my part be appropriate in the light of the Gospel?" (This is not a morbid thought but one meant to put our life and day in perspective in light of our finite nature.)

3. They read Scripture at night or sometime during the day but they read it with a sense of surprise. Again, in the words of James Fenhagen, "The question we ask is simple: What is it about this passage of the Bible that suggests a new way of viewing the world, or forces us to see differently?"

These steps, while not being the be-all, end-all, are designed to help us transform our day so that it all becomes holy. Prayer and reflection are not a call to do more but to be more. If we can see our whole day—work, play, at home, in church, at the supermarket—as being God's day, then we will not separate our lives into two parts: our part and God's part. But we will look for God and bring God everywhere—from our interactions with our families in the morning to the chance meetings with our neighbors, to the interactions we have with our co-workers, to the community worship we have on Sunday. Remember, it is both possible to do many, many so-called good things and not be living in the Spirit of

Holiness, just as it is possible to live a life molded by the Lord that appears ordinary to all who look on. The difference is in our outlook: is it molded by us or God?

Special Personalities: The Value Of Uniqueness

We meet many people in life whom we respect and would like to emulate. We may even wish we were one of them. We may see talented and seemingly self-assured people and we think: "Why can't I be like them?" We may see other persons doing what we perceive to be important things and think: "What am I doing with my life? What special contributions am I making?"

Such fleeting negative references to ourselves, while natural, need to be recognized and addressed when they appear. Such negative thoughts about ourselves fly in the face of the fact that as people we are created in the image and likeness of God; our talents are actually the footprints of God. Thus, the question we should be asking ourselves is not how can we be like someone else, but what is blocking us from becoming who we are destined to become in the eyes of God.

The Rabbi Zusya said a short time before his death, "In the world to come, I shall not be asked, 'Why were you not Moses?' Instead, I shall be asked, 'Why were you not Zusya?' " So, rather than wasting energy on worrying about past time wasted and what "special" things you can accomplish in the future, look at yourself as you are now and ask yourself what special gifts God has already given you.

E. E. Cummings said, "To be nobody but yourself in a world which is doing its best, night and day, to make you everybody else—means to fight the hardest battle which any human being can fight, and never stop fighting." The essence of this fight is to see your personality style for what it is, rejoice in its presence, and see under what circumstances you "trip over" your style. For instance, if you are a sensitive person, that's great! There are so many callous people in this world, thank the Lord for your presence. However, there is a cross to bear with this talent —as there is with every talent or personality style. Sensitive people sometimes become negatively oversensitive; thus, they hear praise in a whisper and negative comments as thunder. When this happens, the sensitive person should become aware of it and ask: "Why am I giving more credence to the negative than the positive?"

Another personality style is the organized person. This style also is quite needed, especially in religious community living. Each local religious community, to function effectively, needs three types of people: the evaluator, who asks: "Did we do what we said we were going to do as a Christian community?"; the visionary, who asks: "What should we be doing in the future?"; and the organizer, who asks: "Did we take out the garbage?" Yet, the organized person can go astray too. In such instances, the person focuses too much on the details and forgets the overall picture (what we call the *gestalt*). In such cases, instead of being an effective organizer, the person becomes rigidly involved with specifics.

So, in the eyes of God, and psychologically, we all have special personalities. The important goal for us should be avoiding tripping over our style through becoming more aware of who we are and who we are becoming. To do this, rather than trying to become—or wishing we were —someone else, we should take out time each day to reflect on who we are being called to be. One way to do this is to ask: "What do people whom I respect like about me?" If you are cheerful and supportive and that's what they like then try to continue that behavior while keeping a wary eye on when this behavior becomes a problem for you; for example, you try to cheer up others and support them but never take out time to receive support from others. In this way, each day can be a time for you to become more self-aware and better able to reach out to others. And, in doing this you will be better in touch with the special part you play in creating the mosaic we call "The People of God."

Forgiveness

Forgiveness is important for both spiritual and psychological reasons. It is the cornerstone of our relationship with God. In addition, it is the basis of our ability to learn about ourselves and experience Christ in others.

Since prayer is basically an experience of relationship with God, it is not surprising then that as long as people have a hard time believing they are forgiven, they are also having a hard time praying. The two—believing God forgives them and having a relationship with the Lord in prayer—go hand in hand.

They say that their head believes they are forgiven but their heart doesn't. Maybe it is more accurate to say that intellectually they can grasp the possibility of being forgiven, but they are coming directly up against their underlying belief that this just isn't so. With this in mind, one part of the answer is to confront the underlying belief they have that they are unworthy persons by admitting it. Then having done this, after meditating and rationalizing intellectually, they should realize that despite this they are loved; or, in the words of Pierre-Marie Delfieux:

"Even should your heart condemn you, God is greater than your heart." This is graphically portrayed in the New Testament by both Judas and Peter. Both let Jesus down; however Judas could not believe in God's forgiveness and was in despair, whereas Peter could conceive of it and became a cornerstone of the Church.

Psychologically, forgiveness is of great value, too. It enables us to be open to our mistakes and failings without anxiety. When we fall we can learn. In addition, in our appreciation of both our sinfulness and God's great love we can then approach others not as people who are lost, and not as the self-righteous who are saved by our own efforts, but as fellow sinners who seek to learn how we might better receive God's grace.

Also, by psychologically holding onto the mystery of God's great love, we can be open to the Spirit in a way that opens us up to its action in our lives. If we turn to St. John's gospel, we see his portrayal of the Spirit through the use of the word "paraclete." This word means, among other things, "animate," "exhort," and "comfort." By recognizing God's love in our minds and holding it there by our determined will, we can ask in prayer for help to overcome our lack of trust in this love.

C.S. Lewis once noted: " . . . we want to know not how we should pray if we were perfect but how we should pray being as we now are." Therefore, in our prayer we must be honest. We must admit our doubt if this is what we feel, but we also must hold on tightly to our faith. This is one of the best prayers we can make because it is based on truth and humility.

Finally, we should reflect on the following words of Robert Faricy, SJ, contained in a little book I had the pleasure of working on with him entitled *Contemplating Jesus*. In it he says; "Jesus loves me. He does not love me because I am great; he really loves me because I am not. He did not come to save the just. He does not love me in spite of my sinfulness; he loves me partly because of my weakness, sinfulness, frailty; it is a characteristic in me to which he can respond with his compassion. My weakness and sinfulness provide the 'opening' to his salvific love."

Emotionally Blackmailed
By Parents

Adults can still feel like they're five years old when it comes to dealing with their parents. In such instances, they may still be trying to please their parents or proving to them that they really are adults, that they truly are "somebody."

Unfortunately, this problem is all too common. When we are young, the significant people in our lives are usually our parents. In some cases, due to a paucity in personal psychological resources, they treat their children in a way that is not based on acceptance and love. Instead, the love is conditional and the message given is: you are not good unless you do what we want. This message is further complicated by the fact that another message often underlies it. This one says: you will never be able to do what we want.

Since these messages are unconscious ones—most parents are not consciously malicious—and they are often given nonverbally (by a gesture or facial expression), they are first sent preverbally when the child is small and can't speak. Yet, they are imprinted on the child's unconscious.

They stay into adulthood and unconsciously control the person unless they are brought out into the open and dealt with assertively and courageously.

Too often we think we are dealing with these messages when we try to prove to our parents that we are really all right. However, the problem remains that under all of this effort is a loyalty to the original message of the parents: you are not all right—no matter what you do. Consequently, even if we have accomplished a lot and many people applaud us, we still feel like charlatans and we still look to our parents and other rejecting figures in our environment to say that we are all right. The fact is, we are remaining loyal to the original image we were given of ourselves, even though we know intellectually that we are better than we feel—and believe our parents feel—about us.

In these cases, we often feel a gnawing hunger for acceptance and a vacillation between anger and sadness toward the parents we have because we feel cheated that we don't have the parents we deserve. So, at times we absent ourselves from our parents or argue with them. At other times we try to do everything for them so they won't have anything against us and maybe will finally accept us. The whole business is quite confusing, exhausting, and frustrating. The question we seem to ask in such circumstances is: Why can't I accept myself and accept that my parents aren't going to change?

This question may just lead to frustration and the feeling that there is no answer to it. However, in reality it is a good question and deserves to be answered assertively every day. In spite of our feelings (which is really the unconscious negative schema received in childhood), we should dare to accept ourselves. We should proceed in the world as if we were all right because in reality we are! We have to be like a pilot at high altitudes who must be guided by the instruments instead of his eyes. (Pilots who guide the plane by their eyes instead of the instruments at high altitudes can fly upside down even though they believe they are seeing the horizon correctly.) The instruments we must be guided by are the acceptance by our friends and many of our acquaintances and our unconditional acceptance by God. Despite the doubt and turmoil behind this belief, we must hold onto it with our whole being.

The second acceptance must be of our parents. I did not say resignation, I said acceptance. This is an active process of looking at the givens, understanding them, and living within them. By having realistic expectations we no longer look at them in a way that sets us up to be disappointed. It is very, very hard—almost impossible?—to accept the reality that our parents are not (never have been and probably will never completely be in the future —even if they mellow) what we would like them to be. But it is this acceptance of reality, this acceptance of our cross in life, that will set us free to live rather than chase illusions.

The power is in our hands to accept—not in our parents' hands to reform. The sooner this message is grasped and lived without looking back or panicking, the sooner life becomes a reality to be lived instead of an existence to be complained about in sorrow. The result of acceptance is we are able to feel the mother and father love that is all around us in our friends and acquaintances and even in the realistic glimmers that may appear from our parents. But first reality must be faced directly, and this is what most of us shy away from because we hold onto a sense of justice rather than a deep sense of love; the love by which we accept ourselves and life in whatever form we see it.

Adult Children Of Alcoholics

We are all affected in many different way by things that happen to us as children. Therefore, if an alcoholic parent were present in the home during the formative years, it is logical for a child to be psychologically impacted in some way. There has been some specific discussion recently concerning the therapeutic issues of adult children of alcoholics.

This information is important not as a way of sending guilt trips upon formerly or currently alcoholic parents, or to excuse irresponsible behavior in the adult children of alcoholics themselves, but to help all concerned understand some of the problems people who had alcoholic parents may be experiencing now. By understanding such difficulties, they can then be dealt with in an efficient manner. Moreover, there seems to be strong evidence now that there is a serious danger that persons who grew up in a family with at least one alcoholic parent are at considerable risk of marrying an alcoholic, or developing certain inappropriate interpersonal styles or psychological difficulties.

This information is important to realize—not as a scare tactic—but to ensure that the issue is out in the open so the chances of these problems continuing are lessened. And one of the best ways to do this is to discuss the topic openly.

In many cases this is difficult to do because when the adult child of an alcoholic was very young, coping behaviors were learned that are not helpful now. As a child the person with an alcoholic parent(s) may have dealt with the stress, confusion, and chaos in the house by denying the problem and being overresponsible (a "parentified child"). As a result, when such a child gets older, it is normal for him or her to continue the denial and loyalty to the parents by avoiding discussion and healthy ventilation of the feelings that have long been pent up and repressed.

Yet, discussion of the past and a heightened awareness of some of the problems being experienced in the present by adult children of alcoholics are essential if the key issues that the person needs to face now are to surface. Such discussion may take place in counseling or therapy, but they can also be undertaken successfully in some instances as part of an Al-Anon organized self-help group.

Not only past experiences come to the surface in such groups, but there is an opportunity to see one is not alone and to appreciate the common themes and experiences of growth that others have had. In such settings, as in therapy, questions around trust and assertiveness are grappled with and faced. Strategies to increase self-esteem, accept the reality of the past, and challenge possibilities of the present and future are also viewed.

To learn more about this topic or to find out where the nearest A-C-O-A group is meeting, anyone interested should contact the local alcoholism information center, alcoholism and addictions council, or Alcoholics Anonymous.

Problem Drinking and Unemployment: Answers Do Exist

A common problem that affects many couples today is—problem drinking due to unemployment. The following hypothetical case will serve as an illustration: A man who worked steadily in a trade recently has been only able to get part-time work at minimum wage. Since this type of income and the lack of benefits are inadequate, he has sought other jobs. Yet, when he looks for work, the only response he gets from prospective employers is, "Fill out an application; we'll look it over and call you." But they never do. To make matters worse, he has a drinking problem. So when he doesn't get a job he turns to alcohol to "solve" his problem. His wife has a hard time with this. Yet, even when she tells him he needs help, he denies it. And the problem continues.

Unemployment and problem drinking are common bad companions. When people have dedicated so many of their years to a certain industry and the rug is pulled out from under them, it is quite a blow to both self-esteem and the financial stability of the family. Unfortunately, this unfair movement to replace long-time steady employees with part-time ones at minimum wage is present in more and more industries today. The negative impact on persons in their 50s and 60s is devastating. Consequently, turning to an "old friend" (alcoholic beverages) who was part of celebrations in better times is not unusual. Naturally though, this only compounds the problem.

During periods of unemployment, drinking encourages denial and brings on nostalgia. Neither help. A clear head and seeking some kind of income are difficult when heavy drinking is involved. Alcohol provides temporary comfort and a guarantee of long-term problems . . . not only for the husband but for the wife as well.

The serious danger is that the wife may give up and let the situation provide a slow martyrdom for her. There *are* things that couples such as these can do. First, the direct approach with problem drinkers rarely works when they are in the denial stage; however, for the wife to sit back and let the situation continue to destroy her is also not the answer. Consequently, I suggest that such spouses call Al-Anon (Alcoholics Anonymous). They usually have a 24 hours a day phone-in service. They will be able to discuss the problem over the phone and put the spouse in touch with a person, like herself, who can guide her on how to deal with the situation and preserve her sanity. She shouldn't avoid doing this; she must get the support and information she needs.

Second, if the husband hasn't tried it as yet, he should approach the county department of vocational rehabilitation. They usually have an employment service, which is part of an approach that includes vocational/growth counseling. He probably has talents from previous jobs that he can use in other areas. The wife should encourage him to move ahead in this direction and support him wherever possible, AND also seek the help and support she needs. Concerned spouses must tie faith and action together by not delaying on such matters.

Make Confrontation a Positive, Christian Force

Confrontation and Christianity seem to make such terrible companions. In many settings, confrontation is absent, indirectly undertaken, or inappropriately manifested as the "holy interpersonal hammer" of God. These realities are unfortunate not only because people are hurt when they are crushed by ill-planned confrontations but also because they are deprived when they are not confronted in those situations where they should be if they are to continue to grow in Christ.

In a book for those in active ministry Ralph Underwood notes: "To move beyond borders of empathy to consider confrontation in pastoral ministry may appear to be like entering an alien land. The difference is striking. In empathic listening, the pastor's own viewpoint is held in check to assure accurate and caring understanding of the other person. In confrontation, a perspective other than the parishioner's own is introduced. Usually empathy helps people expand and develop what they themselves have introduced. While one may hope for readiness, confrontation ventures to help persons face facts or issues they may not want to consider.... Respect is a moral connection that discloses how empathy and certain ways of being confrontive require each other.

"Respectful, considerate confrontation goes hand in hand with empathy. This is not the kind of confrontational attitude where one says, 'It's my job to hit people between the eyes with reality, and what they do with it is their business'. Rather, respectful confrontation communicates in essence, 'Having gained some understanding of you, I now trust you to deal openly with some things you have not considered'. That is, for all their differences, there is no fundamental contradiction when ministers who are empathic are also confrontational, so long as there is respect. Such an understanding of pastoral ministry is critical, if pastors are to be faithful to Christian tradition, including its ethical dimensions . . . .By listening, pastors adapt themselves to others. When this posture is not balanced by challenging persons to consider others' perspective, it runs the risk of encouraging people to idolize their own self-understanding . . . Confrontation, then, invites persons to extend and enrich their participation in community."

Although written for those in pastoral ministry, the above comment can be made to every one of us. However, knowing that confrontation is an essential aspect of communication and knowing when and how to do it are two different things. Although the topic can be quite complex and the issue of confrontation is a delicate one, some basic points can be made about it as a way of introducing the idea.

First of all, respect is essential. Confrontation without it will result in a mere victimizing of the person. Second, we must—as part of this respect—be willing to confront the person as an equal. By that I mean that there must be an openness to change our views, confront our own feelings, thoughts, and ways of viewing the world, as we help others confront theirs; not to be open to this simultaneous confrontation is to be closed, defensive, and lacking of the model of willingness to grow that we are asking of those whom we are confronting.

Third, we should have developed a trusting relationship with the person so that they can believe we have listened to them, understood them, and are empathic to where they are with respect to the issue in question.

Fourth, in confrontation, we should be specific and unpretentious in our approach. With respect to specificity, to quote Professor Underwood again: "Concreteness anchors understanding, intensifies it, and prepares a person for genuine change in identifiable ways. General insights foster self-satisfaction and produce little change." If we deal with a specific issue, a general conclusion and application can often be made; however, if we are too vague, then we are often left with a general insight that never seems to apply in reality. In terms of unpretentiousness, confrontation should be made as part of the natural interaction between two people (sinners) walking together to God rather than a professional helpful dictum from on high. Here our attitude toward ourselves is just as important as our respect for others.

Fifth, our observations that are confrontational should be presented in a tentative fashion. In this way, the person being confronted can participate in confronting the situation or perspective. Such mutuality helps in convincing the person of the reality of our respect.

Sixth, in confronting we need to own our contribution to the issue being dealt with; not to do so is to deny that relationships are dynamic and involve all participants. Such self-disclosure about our own part breaks down the barrier between the confronter and the person being faced with an issue. The situation becomes more mutually open, satisfying, and growthful.

Confrontation isn't easy. We often are anxious about conflict. Sometimes we use it as a method of revenge rather than help. Other times people misunderstand and think ill of us because of our candor. And still other times, we are not clear and respectful and thus mess up the encounter. However, even given all of this, confrontation is necessary if Christian community is to remain alive and growthful. The goal in Christian confrontation is to encourage people to be all they can be without embarrassing them as to who they are and what they are doing in life. Since we are all human we will occasionally miss the mark; yet, with respect for others and a willingness to be open ourselves, confrontation can open up new opportunities to receive God's grace.

Powerful Negative Thinking (And Other Faulty Thinking Patterns)

People accuse many of us of being too negative. They say we never see the bright side and that we have a bad attitude. We may agree but sometimes can't help feeling insecure. We are bothered when things go wrong and are very sensitive to the negative things others associate with us. People may say this is because we have a bad self-image and suggest we raise our self-esteem.

Negative thinking is not unusual. Most of us are trained for some reason to give more credence to the negative than to the positive. We can hear many, many positive things but somehow allow one negative comment to discolor and disqualify the previously affirming feedback we have gotten. It's as though we dwell on the single negative detail until it becomes so large that it blacks out reality. We need to recognize when we do this so we can stop and replace the negative self-talk we have with more realistic comments. In this way we don't automatically accept the common nonsense we are saying about ourselves as if it were common sense.

In picking up negative thinking and trying to correct it, it might also be of help if we could recognize a number of other faulty thinking patterns:

1. *Inappropriate generalizations and magnifications:* we see a single undesirable occurrence or specific negative event as representing a pattern or symbolic of something more terrible than it really is. (e.g., A person disagrees with us or is emotionally "grumpy," and we believe it is evidence that they don't like us or we are an unlikeable person.)

2. *Black-and-white thinking:* if we don't achieve all of our goals or reach the perfectionistic objective we have set out, we feel like a failure.

3. *Negative mind reading:* we believe we can see the negative without evidence. Therefore, we anticipate negative results or assume people are thinking or acting negatively without having evidence or attempting to check it out.

4. *Uncritical acceptance of negative feelings:* we accept our negative feelings as if they are based on something true rather than trying to uncover the negative—often faulty—thinking underlying them.

Faulty thinking, in general, is the nemesis at the source of many of our negative feelings about ourselves. Even if we have been a so-called negative or hypersensitive person all our lives and have let any disruption or unpleasant happening cause us turmoil, this can be changed. The important initial step is to pick up this negative thinking and answer it assertively rather than accepting the unexamined assumptions as true.

Part of the excitement of the Christian life is that we can believe that we are accepted, really accepted and loved by God . . . if we doubt it we need only look up at the crucifix and see the fact of it. This trust in our forgiveness and being loved should be a basis for a continual appreciation of the gift we can be to people when we don't uncritically accept the negative as being more true than the positive. The rule of thumb is: learn from the negative—don't exaggerate it or beat yourself up with it. Self-love and self-examination should go hand in hand; when they do we can be, as children say today, an "awesome" presence for good rather than being tied up in unnecessary negative preoccupation, self-doubt, and self-criticism.

He Has Everything...
He's Never Happy

All of us probably know the type of person who is a real "go-getter" and has gotten far in business. Bright and energetic, warm, trustworthy, and dependable, he may be a senior executive with a major company, around 50, and financially quite well off. Yet, he doesn't seem very happy, everything seems to annoy him.

This type of person may well be experiencing "male menopause." Yet, even if he isn't, many males in this age group, whether executives or not, become frustrated, feel exploited, and lose their appreciation for life. It is a function of increased age, decreased opportunities, and the many psychological, physiological, and social changes taking place in their lives.

Accordingly, it is not unusual to hear men or women in this group saying such things as:

- "They (children, friends, co-workers) don't appreciate me."

- "I feel like I'm hitting my head against the wall. The harder I work, the less money I have (or the less I accomplish)."

- "I'm getting tired of doing the same things; life just isn't as much fun anymore."

Along with the attitude problem reflected by the comments noted above, increased use of alcohol and a reduced ability to creatively enjoy leisure time result. The man often pulls back from even his spouse because he feels misunderstood. In such a case, the wife often complains she is in a no-win situation. If she tries to point out his inappropriate thinking or hypersensitivity, he gets angry and says she's not on his side. On the other hand, if she tries to ignore his outbursts and remains quiet, he accuses her of not caring about him. The situation seems hopeless.

The approach I have taken is to agree with the man that he does indeed deserve more out of life. Then I proceed to examine with him what he can do to become more alive, more receptive of what life still has to offer. The goal is to accept the right of the person to experience joy while helping him to examine, understand, and change those behaviors that are interfering with an appreciation of life.

In response to this, most men in this category still remain defensive and declare it is not their fault that their attitude is poor. When this happens, I agree with them that it isn't totally their problem; however, I also emphasize that when the blame is projected out onto someone else, the power is given away as well. The question when facing any problem is: What can I do to affect my destiny?

For instance, with respect to his children, the man at this age may feel he has done so much for them that they owe him. This debt is then translated into an unrealistic expectation that they will meet his (often abruptly changeable) needs and respond completely to his unspoken requests. In such a case, by adjusting his expectations, seeing what he has done for his children in the past more in the sense of *mitzvah* (giving without expecting anything in return). Being more clear about his needs and requests, he will often get more of his key expectations met and be less frustrated, thus enjoying their presence more and making his children more interested in being with him.

In terms of his feeling frustrated financially or occupationally, efforts need to be taken to assist him to step back and actively try to be open to the joys that are already present now in his life. We all buy the world's version as to what success is to some extent. The 40s and 50s are ideal times to pull back from being duped . . . this is a time to stop comparing ourselves with those whom we see have more and to begin to appreciate life less in quantity and more in quality. Too often we have confused quality of life with quantity of life and spent our waking moments chasing some image of success that we have been sold by the media instead of God.

The essential goal then is to help the man in this position to realize that it is natural to experience some sense of loss and frustration at this age. Yet, these limits can lead to greater creativity and depth, which will uncover new ways of appreciating life. So instead of living under the tyranny of this stage, drawing into himself, or ventilating without doing anything, the development of a new way of relating to self, the world, and God is the route to take to receive the most satisfaction. Assertiveness, being more open to positive comments, greater flexibility, and development of new skills are all waiting for the person who can let go of old expectations of self and others.

Finally, if the person is not willing to let go, patience on the part of those close to him and/or several sessions of growth counseling would seem to be the best current approach open. Growth can't be forced on someone, so close friend or relatives must keep that in mind while they're trying to have an impact on him. Otherwise there will be two people frustrated and that, while understandable, is really unnecessary and should be avoided by being realistic in the goals one sets in dealing with him.

Emotional Difficulties and Hope

When suffering from fears, irrational thoughts, or some other mental stress, there is a good deal of tension and anxiety present. Under such circumstances it is natural to question our faith and to wonder if there's something we are doing wrong.

Psychologically, if we get a thought that says, "I am not a good person and not trying hard enough," we should reject it totally as irrational and know that we are trying as hard as is humanly possible. Spiritually, if we ever doubt whether we will continue to get better, we must remember Jesus' words in John's Gospel, "I will not leave you orphaned."

Even in the tough times, the times we feel in turmoil and bound up with tension, we know that God is with us; and in those times we do feel a bit more relaxed and at ease, we should rejoice in the Lord. In our prayer, we must picture a warm, loving God who trusts us and is satisfied with us and wants us to relax. Whenever we feel ourselves tightening up and our thoughts or fears running away with us, we should bring this image to mind. With the support of our families, a physician if necessary, and God, we'll make it. We must have faith and remember Jesus' words, "Be not afraid."

Emotional problems, like mental stress, can also be overwhelming. A specific sexual problem, for example, might make us turn to the media for some general advice. Although advice in a newspaper column or from a radio or TV show can be helpful, there is no substitute for personal professional help regarding a specific problem. Such a problem needs to be discussed with a physician or a priest. Once we have seen a physician and still wish counseling, we should present the problem to our priest, in writing if we choose, and ask him for a time when we can discuss the issue in confidence.

As to the confidential nature of such inquiry, we might choose to contact the priest under the anonymity that is the proper right of a penitent. For example, the writer could send his inquiry unsigned to his pastor to give a written answer, which he would stop to pick up, say, on next Saturday afternoon in the confessional.

Priests, as called leaders of the Christian community, are present to be consultants on issues that touch matters of faith, so all of us should avail ourselves of this help in times of mental or emotional stress.

Worrying

Even when everything seems to be going well in life, many of us can't resist searching for something to worry about or blowing things out of proportion. We seem to be constantly preoccupied with the negative. We may recognize that this style is unproductive and want to do something about it, but it can be difficult when we've been this way all our lives.

Worrying is such a serious drain on our energy level. We also realize that it is a waste of energy. In addition, worriers turn people off. Who wants to be near a person whose implicit philosophy of life is negative? In the extreme, worriers are like "silver linings" always looking for the clouds.

However, this style can be altered. Just because people have been this way for most of their lives is not an insurmountable problem. Every personality style has a positive and negative side and there is but a fine line dividing the two. Often the other side of the line is to be a concerned person.

Concerned people are great. They see the issues, they are

sensitive to others, and they can appreciate some of the factors in their own lives that need attention. However, the difference between the worrier and the concerned person is the attitude.

The worrier's style is based on anxiety and the desire to control; the concerned person's style is based on reality and the ability to trust. Based on this difference, the worrier becomes *preoccupied* and ruminates over problems, whereas the concerned person becomes *occupied* with the problem and plans or acts in accordance with an assessment of it.

Henri Nouwen, in his brief, clear book on the spiritual life, *Making All Things New*, addresses this problem directly when he says: "To be preoccupied means to fill our time and place long before we are there. This is worrying in the more specific sense of the word. It is a mind filled with 'ifs'. We say to ourselves, 'What if I get the flu? What if I lose my job? What if my child is not home on time? What if there is not enough food tomorrow? What if a war starts? What if the world comes to an end? What if . . . ?' All these 'ifs' fill our minds with anxious thoughts and make us wonder constantly what to do and what to say in case something should happen in the future. Much, if not most, of our suffering is connected with these preoccupations."

What can we do then if we are a worrier? How can we transform our preoccupations? The approach we need to use is as much tied to our spirituality as it is to our psychology. We must try to consciously increase our trust in the Lord as much as we try to let go psychologically of those things we cannot control. So, the steps we can take each day are:

1. We should say a morning prayer for trust in the Lord . . . a belief that he will stand with us no matter

what we face. Also, we must recollect this desire during the middle of the day and as we go to sleep.

2. When a worry comes up, we should occupy ourselves with it instead of preoccupy ourselves with it; we should break down the problem and plan on an approach rather than ruminate on its sad or negative qualities and focus on our helplessness.

3. We should then limit ourselves as to how long we will spend on coming up with a strategy so we don't let it fill our entire day.

4. Finally, we should avoid the "savior complex" by recognizing our limits and the Lord's limitless power. In a sense we should stop taking ourselves seriously and begin taking the Lord more seriously in prayer.

So, if we do this, then we can address real concerns directly and not let unnecessary pain (neurotic worrying) make the situation worse. Thus, when a friend or relative is sick or dying, we can face the issue by praying, appreciating the gift of our own health, planing on how we can be present to the person, and seeking to find with the person God's gentle presence amidst the pain of the situation.

Joy and Laughter

John Catoir, Director of the Christophers, in his famous book *Enjoy the Lord*, said: "After years of counseling priests, sisters, mothers, fathers and teenagers, I came to realize how difficult it is for most people to be joyful. Life isn't easy and there are always problems to weigh us down. On the other hand, we were made for joy and there is in us a human faculty tuned to God's inner life of total joyfulness. It is the soul."

Being sensitive to the injustices in the world is an important part of being Christian. Yet, if we are to do this in an ongoing way, we must also have a theology of hope that trusts ultimately in the Lord. So, although we are being called to recognize, speak out against, and fight injustice, we must also appreciate that amidst all of this thought and action, God is with us. This contemplative attitude of living enables us to be joyful and peaceful. It also makes us recognize that in facing the tough spots of life, we are not being called to solve all the problems. Instead we are being asked to face them with the joyful knowledge that God is with us when we are compassionate. People are not saints because they worry more or are bet-

ter activists; they are saints because the truth they speak
and the actions they take emanate out of a joyful, gentle
contact with God.

Psychologically, such joyfulness is tied very much to an
accurate picture of ourselves. Such a picture is formed
when we take out the time each day to quietly pray. It is
also formed through laughter. Norman Cousins, who
wrote the book *Anatomy of an Illness* and was the only
layperson to my knowledge ever to get an article pub-
lished in the *New England Journal of Medicine,* said that
laughter helped him during the period when he battled
with a chronic disease. He said that he would watch a
comedy show on TV for about 10 minutes and that the
belly laughter had an anesthetic effect on him. Following
the laughter he could lie down and get two hours of pain-
free sleep. From this he deduced that laughter is good
medicine. The same can be said about laughter at ourselves (e.g., gently kidding ourselves when we become too
inflated or serious). If laughter is good medicine, surely
laughing at ourselves must truly be healing. As human
beings we have the gift of laughter—this is one of our dis-
tinguishing marks in the animal kingdom. Yet, more
often than not we avoid using this gift to enjoy life's
quirks and tease ourselves into recognizing that while we
need to face our responsibilities, we care not alone . . . we
are made for joy.

The final point is with respect to the importance of
detachment. The late Urban Holmes III said in his book
Spirituality for Ministry: "Detachment means our freedom from being victimized by our own emotions and
those to whom we minister. The opposite of detachment
is not compassion, it is seduction." In the above statement
Dr. Holmes is cautioning us not to try to meet the expectations of others that are unrealistic (that we can completely cure the problem in one hour) and our own

unrealistic expectations (that we should be the saviour rather than someone who is trying to do something good in behalf of the saviour). Instead, the implication of his statement is that we should only try to meet God's expectations, which is to do what we can to reveal the Lord's healing presence by what we do, how we react, and—of most importance—what attitude we display to others in need.

Perfectionism, Psychology, Prayer

Perfectionists often feel as if they're driving themselves crazy. As Christians they believe this is part of doing the best they can. Yet, being so intense need not be part of a movement toward God.

Wanting to be the best is a worthy and necessary goal. However, the way persons view the goal, rather than the goal itself, can be the source of difficulties. Rather than perfection being a goal that inspires people to be the best they can, it may be one that is threatening them and making them feel they are not good enough.

In psychological jargon, many perfectionists are "shoulds" persons who experience a self-esteem problem. From a spiritual perspective, they may place themselves in front of a super-ego-oriented God who is saying to them that they are bad, sinful, and not pleasing to him.

One way they can deal with this is by taking out a few minutes for morning meditation to put themselves in front of an ego-oriented God, i.e., a God who is calling them in love to be all they can be, one who knows failure is part of living a full Christian life. In doing this, their

Perfectionism, Psychology, Prayer

failures won't be seen as evidence that they are bad, but merely as human blocks to finding Christ within themselves and others. In this light, failures are seen as opportunities to learn about oneself and appreciate dependence on God; they are not occasions for self-condemnation. Thus the trouble with respect to perfectionism is: when their goals inspire persons, the result is a high degree of motivation; when goals only serve to threaten them, the result is unnecessary depression and turmoil.

★ ★ ★

I would just like to conclude this short essay by addressing those who want to learn to pray or who want to find out more about praying. The following three books may be of some help:

- Anthony Bloom, _Beginning to Pray_ (Paulist Press)
- Henri Nouwen, _Making All Things New_ (Harper & Row)
- Richard Hauser, _In His Spirit_ (Paulist Press)

If your bookstore doesn't have these books, ask the manager to order them for you. Most bookstores would be happy to special order books for a customer. After reading one or more of them, you might find it helpful to speak with someone about your impressions of the material. In this regard, contacting a spiritual director, speaking with a parish priest or director of religious education, calling a local retreat center for an appointment with one of its personnel, or joining a prayer group might be a good idea.

Praying for Strength

In times of trial some people pray for God's intervention with a rigid set of expectations as to what God should do. In most cases they want the status quo to be reestablished by God; in other words, if they have lost health, money, job, etc., they want God to intervene and return it to them. Still others ask God for help in a situation but in their hearts they really don't want help in the form of assistance; they want to be rescued. By this I mean that they want God to come down, go into the midst of the difficult situation while they wait in the background unscathed. It's like they're saying to God, "You walk point into the battle and get crucified but I'll be right behind you so I can be there in time for the resurrection."

The alternative to the above styles of lament, however, shouldn't be to go it alone. To do so would be dangerous because we would be distancing ourselves from God, failing to develop a sound spirituality/theology of hope, and building up the illusion that we actually can handle life's crises beneficially by ourselves. The fact is we need God. When we don't call upon him, we run the risk of falling into despair, confusion, skepticism, or a self-reliance that can easily grow into self-worship.

Crises are mysteries in which we can find God and grow, but they are also times when we can despair and move away from him. In prayer we need to ask him for strength, to stand with us, and to help us uncover his love amidst the pain. When faced with pain, we should have low expectations (which are based on what we want) but high hopes (which are based on what we and God together can achieve in love.)

Too often what prevents us from finding God amidst life's pain is a concentration on its cause. We ask, "Why is this happening to me? What did I do to deserve this?" In such instances, we seem to be blaming God for our troubles. If we follow this feeling to its logical conclusion, we are then left with two negative possibilities: either God is heartless or we are very guilty and deserving of punishment. Therefore, if we or someone we love gets cancer, either God doesn't love us or we have done something wrong to merit this pain. Naturally, this is far from the truth.

The world in its freedom has been given the gifts of water and air, and in its freedom it has polluted them. From such sources people are bound to get sick. When this happens, prayer for strength and healing is appropriate and needed. The answer may come in the form of an obvious miracle—physical healing. However, we must also be open to other answers from God. During the mystery of pain, some people ask for help and listen only to the miracle they are seeking. If it doesn't come, they feel abandoned. Others in pain ask for help and are open to it in any form it comes; they open their ears to the Spirit and they hear God. Their faith is strengthened.

We must try to join the latter group and seek God everyday, even in our pain and confusion. As Rabbi Kushner points out in his book *When Bad Things Happen to Good People,* it is not the source of pain but the result of it that is important; the outcome for some is bitterness, while the result for others is growth. How we seek God is the key. And, the fidelity in which we see Christ as the door, is the Way.

Spiritual Growth, Marital Discord—Part 1

People who decide to enter the realm of spiritual direction usually find it to be a very rewarding experience. Speaking to someone about their prayer life and relationship with God is a joyful experience. However, this new calling can sometimes cause some friction at home. A spouse may tease the person about becoming a "Holy Roller" or say the person pays too much attention to God and not enough attention to him or her. The person in spiritual direction may be at a loss about how to handle the problem

Change, any type of change—be it good or bad— causes some degree of stress. One of the reasons a spouse probably reacts is merely due to this alteration in the other spouse's habits. Also, when getting involved in something new, it is natural that energy is siphoned off from other areas, even if it is only minimal in terms of the amount of time being spent.

Another possible cause for reaction is that the husband or wife may be threatened by the other's relationship with the spiritual director and the possibility that their outlook in life might be altered by their involvement in a disciplined prayer life. This, too, is not unusual and has a parallel for people who enter counseling or psychotherapy. In the case of counseling, spouses often feel somewhat competitive with the counselor and initially worry about what impact the treatment will have on the equilibrium in the marital relationship. In most cases, when they see the positive results, the concern lessens and is more apt to be replaced by some good-natured kidding about the whole process.

One of the ways in which this stress can be lessened is by informing a spouse as to what exactly spiritual direction is; this process in itself should help diffuse some of the anxiety and stress. By simply noting that spiritual direction is a process in which someone on a regular basis (1x/month, 4x/year, 2x/year . . .) helps a person focus on his or her relationship with God, it is possible to understand that the relationship with the director is not the important element. The relationship with God is. The person who is the director is a knowledgeable person we feel comfortable with, not a friend who we are turning to as a way of filling an interpersonal void in our life.

Another way for spouses in areas such as spiritual direction to prevent undue stress is by looking at their own comments and behavior. If spiritual direction is having a good impact, then they will be modeling healthy behavior. They won't be moving about in their family and elsewhere trying to proselytize people. Such actions don't call people to be all they can by seeing the peace, direction, and enthusiasm it brings the person in spiritual direction; rather they merely reflect the person's own insecurity and need for affirmation that he or she is indeed on the right road. The goal we have as Christians is to attract people to Christ and encourage them to develop into who they can be while not embarrassing them because they are where they are at this point in life.

If anything, spiritual direction should actually enrich a marriage in the long run. Being drawn more and more to God, the person will be drawn more and more to the community of Christ here on earth, of which the spouse is at the heart. Naturally then, if the person finds they are spending more and more time in church, and less and less time with spouse and family, this sounds less like an indication that his prayer life is becoming deeper than it does that he is withdrawing from life inappropriately. (In such instances, a tendency like this needs to be discussed with the spiritual director.)

Being aware of all of the above is important so as not to cause any undue stress or move on an artificial, pietistical road to God. It is also important to know these facts so we can deal with the one reality-based pressure that probably will come from spiritual direction. This pressure results from the changes in vision we are apt to have due to spiritual growth.

(Part 2 of this essay, "Spiritual Growth, Personal Vision," completes this discussion and is presented next.)

Spiritual Growth, Personal Vision—Part 2

(The previous essay, "Spiritual Growth, Marital Discord," focused on how to minimize some of the forms of stress that may result when one spouse enters spiritual direction. Part 2 of this discussion on spiritual development and interpersonal distress concentrates on an important problem that may occur as a result of one person's spiritual growth: an alteration of personal vision that throws off the equilibrium of the family outlook.)

If there is one word that probably summarizes the message we give our children and adolescents as they grow up it is: *accomplish!* This word is often translated by the person entering young adulthood, with the help of a consumer-oriented society, into two words: *consume* and *compete!*

These words then mark the theme for many adults as they enter marriage and the workplace. The big job, the big house, the big salary are the music that go with the lyrics saying: winning is essential, being number one is success, and being known and powerful is the only joint goal worth seeking in life.

Fortunately for us, the Church, the Bible, and the humanists in society eventually help modify these messages. We begin to see the importance of thinking of our neighbor in concrete ways (i.e., sharing money, clothing, and food) and in viewing our neighbors in a broader context (i.e., the "global village" where we are citizens with all peoples of the world of the Kingdom of God.). However, despite these moderations in outlook, we still focus primarily on ourselves, our jobs, our homes, our vacations, and our future security (having a million dollars in our Keogh retirement fund). Spiritual direction and development can possibly alter that, and this is where the conflict can begin.

Spiritual growth can radically impact one's personal vision and thus unsettle the previous equilibrium of the family outlook. For instance, let's take the case of Bill Johnson (a fictitious name). He is a corporate executive with a wife and two children. Up to this point he has been very competitive and security minded. His wife is very content with this; her satisfaction comes from feeling secure in his accomplishments and high income. The big house and portfolio and the children tucked away in private schools all are part of the picture.

The focus of the family, up to this point, has been where they will move next, what promotion he will attain, and how early and on what salary he will retire. Then Bill begins to take a step back and examine his life (in this case maybe without the aid of a director, per se). He decides to take out time for daily prayer in solitude with God in the morning, do a short reflection in the afternoon, and do some scriptural/theological reading in the evening for about 30 minutes. Although this sounds "harmless"—after all, how could a little religion hurt?— and even though he has no dramatic conversion (born again) experience, he begins to question his life and his goals. It's not that he wants to stop being a corporate executive; it's not that he stops wanting to live comfortably; it's not that he doesn't still want the best education possible for his two children. But, his vision has changed.

Instead of being able to sit down and envision a bigger house and retirement fund, he may want a smaller house. Instead of concerning himself with whom they should entertain to increase his chances for advancing his career path, he may want to interact with those whom he believes will challenge him to be all he can be *in the eyes of Christ.* The result? The spouse (and this scenario can be reversed in terms of gender) is confused, conflicted, and not sure whether they share the same vision anymore.

It is at this point that communication, patience with each other, and the guidance of an experienced director or counselor familiar with this natural outcome for spiritual development would be of help. The only danger is either to panic or disregard the feelings and beliefs of either party. Prior to a revisioning in the marriage there is always confusion, and with growth there is always some pain. And, the alternatives—a marriage formed by a philosophy that doesn't have God as its center or one that is not alive—although they may seem better because they provide temporary peace, are surely not to be desired in the long run.

Sex Therapy

Intimacy is the cornerstone of a good marriage. Through conversation, spending time together silently, sharing visions about the marriage, and communicating physically—including sexually—two people are able to develop a special, meaningful, spiritual relationship. Out of the relationship comes love, the kind of love that children, friends, other relatives, and strangers can experience.

Sometimes, due to a lack of knowledge, some experiences in life, or a physical problem, the above intimacy is "short-circuited" physically. As a result, the natural joy of physical communication and sexual intimacy is adversely affected. Consequently, sexual problems (e.g., premature ejaculation, secondary impotence, vaginismus) cause undue and unnecessary pressure on the physical part of the relationship.

Sex therapists are specially educated mental health professionals (psychologists, psychiatrists, etc.). Today most helping professionals have availed themselves of this education, so finding one through a gynecologist, psychologist, or counseling center should not be too difficult. When you go in, a history will be taken and a treatment plan suggested. In each case the approach will include hints on improving communication and understanding. The cure rate is one of the highest in the field of psychology (i.e., for some problems it is 99 + percent).

One of the cornerstones of the approach is something called "sensate focus," which is an exercise that improves physical sensitivity and encourages relaxation. This exercise and the other ones employed generally emanate out of the work of Masters and Johnson and Helen Singer Kaplan. The medically sound, psychologically helpful, and religiously appropriate information provided by these professionals is now in use to help good marriages that are suffering because of sexual difficulties to become stronger.

Probably the biggest caution that can be offered is that sex therapy should not be seen as a solution to a totally incompatible relationship or as a substitute for marriage counseling when there are a number of serious problems (including sexuality) in the relationship. However, where it is indicated, sex therapy can help the Christian couple to move through a physical block to intimacy to the point where it can become even more alive and vital, and thus strengthen family life.

When People Need
Professional Help—Part 1

Probably one of the best ways to arrive at a decision as to whether someone needs professional help or not is by keeping the following questions in mind when you're listening to them relate their difficulties:

- How exaggerated or severe is the behavior or problem being experienced?

- Is the problem or the symptoms very unusual or bizarre in nature?

- Is the person quite baffled as to the cause or solution to the problem?

- How much is the difficulty interfering with the person's overall daily activity?

- Does the behavior seem to be getting worse?

- What has the person already tried in an effort to deal with the problem?

The severity of the problem is one of the keys to knowing whether professional assistance should be sought. Feeling a bit down, anxious, or confused is not cause for alarm in itself. Only when the situation becomes extreme should outside help be given consideration.

A good example of this is the grief reaction. If someone close dies, a person naturally becomes somewhat depressed. This could last for some time, ranging from weeks to possibly months. As a matter of fact, the person, particularly a spouse of 30 or so years, may have short periods of the blues for the rest of his or her life. This is not a cause for undue concern.

However, if the person is severely depressed for month after month, begins developing a number of physical ailments, and doesn't seem to adjust at all, the situation may possibly be abnormal. The key is the severity and duration of the reported symptoms and observable signs. If the reaction is out of proportion with the cause in terms of magnitude or persistence, then it is usually wise to seek outside help to be on the safe side.

The outside help may initially be seeing a physician who can temporarily prescribe a psychotropic drug (one designed to affect behavior or mood), or going to a member of the clergy for support. From that point on, if the problem still persists, then further referral to a psychotherapist may be indicated.

Some examples of the types of situations that might point to the need for a professional mental health evaluation include: persistent, severe depression; overwhelming anxiety; frequent loss of self control (e.g., frequent anger verbally or physically demonstrated without an ability to prevent its expression); incapacitating guilt; extreme hesitancy in dealing with daily problems; continuous preoccupation with personal health; great irrational fears (phobias); persistent marital difficulties; spiraling family problems; inability to adjust to change; excessive drinking, gambling, or use of prescribed or illegal drugs; chronic sleeping or eating problems; inability to develop good interpersonal relationships; difficulty in holding a job; serious school problems; extreme dependency reflected in an inordinate fear of independent, adultlike behavior; great difficulty in relaxing; little ability to concentrate; compelling desire to please others—and the fear of not being able to do so.

In addition to the above, if the person's symptoms are very unusual (e.g., hears voices that are not present in reality, irrationally believes people are plotting against him/her), the person is baffled by the problem, it is getting worse to the point of interfering with his/her daily activities, or nothing done to deal with the problem seems to work, this may also indicate in a general way that professional help is indicated.

(Part 2 of this essay, "Suggesting That People Need Professional Help," completes this discussion and is presented next. For further reading on this topic, see *Helping Others*, available in some libraries or direct from the publisher: Gardner Press, 19 Union Square, New York, NY 10003; $14.95 plus $1.50 postage. In this book I deal with this question and others at greater length.)

Suggesting That People Need Professional Help—Part 2

Telling people that they may need professional help can be an ordeal because of the stigma attached to seeking help in the area of emotional or mental health. Being in therapy can be viewed in very negative or very desirable terms. Some feel that psychotherapy is very chic, particularly if the therapist has the right address, high fees, and a known reputation. For a period of time, and still in some circles, being in analysis with certain professionals was the "in thing." (Also on the positive side is that many people in therapy now are really in it because they are talented and involved. If they weren't so committed and gifted, they wouldn't have become so overwhelmed. I find now that most of my patients are really "stars" who are seeking my help to gain perspective because they have gotten their "psychological fingers" burned because they continue to be on the cutting edge of life.)

On the other end of the spectrum, therapy can be viewed as a real stigma. This is especially the case for some families who view therapy as proof that the person can't work it out on their own and are therefore weak. They never think that the reason the person may be in therapy is to further actualize certain capabilities and strengths that are temporarily stymied.

The family may also object because they see the need for therapy as proof of their own failure. Instead of encouraging a troubled or upset son or daughter to seek outside support, they fight it because they believe if the child goes, it will mean they were failures as parents.

Even the "liberal" segment of our society in many instances harbors mixed feelings about therapy. They may recommend it for others, but if they need it themselves, it's like pulling teeth to get them into it.

Dealing with the blocks a person might have against going into therapy is usually necessary when bringing up the topic with someone. There's no way to get around these potential difficulties and no need to try. However, there are a number of things to keep in mind when recommending outside help for someone:

- Be clear and direct about why you think they should consider asking an expert about the problems they're facing.

- Be clear in your mind about what you want to say before bringing the topic up. Have your own feelings about therapy clear in your mind, too, and be aware *prior* to bringing the topic up of the potential response you may receive. This will reduce the chance that you will seem self-conscious about discussing it and the chance that the other person will feel uncomfortable as a result of your own uneasiness.

- Bring the topic up in a private area. This is a serious and personal issue, and it should be given the privacy and attention it deserves. If the person responds by joking, don't jump in and fool around as well. Some people laugh when they're nervous. You don't want to convey the feeling that you think the problem of emotional distress is a funny or unusual one.

- If pressed about the repugnance of going to a "shrink," the role of a clinical social worker, psychiatrist, or psychologist should be put in the perspective of a specialist in interpersonal relations and mental health. Persons probably wouldn't hesitate to go to a medical specialist or a lawyer, so why should they balk at going to another type of specialist who can possibly facilitate their handling of an issue? One definition of therapy is that it is an intensified version of the normal process of growth.

Reading can be encouraged on the topic. There are a number of books on this subject that can be quite helpful. Refer to the Bibliography at the back of this book for specific titles.

In conducting the discussion in the above manner, while leaving ample room for the person to react and ask questions, the topic of therapy can usually be broached in a very beneficial fashion, with a minimum amount of discomfort for both the helper and the person being helped.

Christian Leadership Isn't Easy

Once, a man was leading an adult group discussion on the topic of spirituality, and two people who disagreed with several of his suggestions for reflection got up and walked out. The group leader later wondered why he even bothered trying to help these people grapple with their spirituality only to take what he saw as abuse. He said that the incident took the joy out of his trying to do the right thing. His feeling was: "It might be better if I just uttered pious platitudes and let them do and think what they want!"

I'm sure that anyone who deals directly with the public, especially in groups, has had this man's experience. The fact that the group is made up of "Christians" does not change that. Actually, at times it may even make it worse, because even though religion attracts the committed, the caring, and the charitable, it also is a magnet for the rigid and the self-righteous.

Another point worth noting is that people often don't realize how much of an impact they have when they are rude and close-minded. I remember giving a series of retreat talks and having people just wander in and out or walk across the room in front of where I was standing and addressing the group. I think they believe it just doesn't matter, probably because they have not been in such a position themselves. The two people who walked out of the room on the group leader probably didn't stop to think of his feelings. If they had, they wouldn't have done something so rude, even if they disagreed with him.

Another mistake we make is to personalize what people do or say to the extent that we make ourselves feel bad when we needn't do so. Again from my own experience I remember being invited to give a brief talk to different groups that met each weekend. When I would pull up in my car I would see people driving away or walking around far from the building where the group was to meet; because of my own crazy thinking I would say to myself, "I guess they don't care about me or don't like my material." Then, it occurred to me that they not only didn't know what I was going to talk about, but they didn't know me. Their behavior was independent of mine, and I was making an erroneous connection between the two.

A final mistake we make is to use what the cognitive psychologists call a "negative filter." We use a negative filter when we inordinately focus on the negative and almost ignore the positive. An example of this is when we get an evaluation of some sort. Many of us tend to gloss over the positive comments, as if they are not important, and concentrate only on the negative ones. In other words, we hear praise in a whisper and criticisms as thunder. Two people may have walked out on the group leader, but many others enjoyed grappling with the issues—issues we should grapple with as long as we belong to the Pilgrim Church that Jesus encouraged us to journey within.

I think in life, particularly in leadership and service positions in the Church, we expect that when we turn the other cheek, people will be so edified by our humility that they will way, "My gosh, look at that humble person; he is so nice and right that I admire him and I will apologize." What really happens is that when we turn the other cheek, psychologically the rigid and the self-righteous take another swing at us.

The pain of Christian leadership isn't easy; while we do embrace in our commitment the peace of Christ, we must also at times carry his cross. Psychologically, however, we should try to lessen the unnecessary pain by: (1) recognizing that working directly with people is stressful so that we are not surprised by the pain; (2) appreciating the fact that people don't know how much they can hurt us through their rudeness and thoughtlessness; (3) not personalizing people's angry comments and actions; and (4) not using a negative filter so we hear the negative more than the positive.

Anger, Leadership, and Feelings Of Failure

One principal shared the following dilemma with me in hopes of finding an answer to the pressures under which she found herself: "I'm the principal of an elementary school. When I was a teacher everyone was afraid of the principal. I have strived to change this attitude by being more open to criticism by parents as well as teachers. However, I'm starting to feel burdened by the anger being dumped on me by others. Did I create a monster by being so willing to hear negative comments?"

Leaders who are closed to criticism are apt to have a distorted view of their organization—be it a school, church, business, or any type of institution/interpersonal team. Ironically, people like this often don't even know they are closing the door to possible negative comments. They may forestall criticism by minimizing it, reacting sharply, viewing it as disloyalty, or being pollyannish when faced with difficulties. The result is a distance between the leader and those under her or him. In addition, a lack of group vitality and generally poor morale are expected common outcomes as well.

Yet, when one does open the door interpersonally, anger and negativity, as well as all of the positive elements that come with openness, can and usually do result. The answer when this happens is not to pull back, however, but deal with the negativity in a different way.

First, try not to personalize and absorb the anger or complaint. People who offer criticism may have a good point as to what is wrong; however, if you take it personally and feel they are blaming you, you will be defensive. Separate the complaint from the complainer and the issue being addressed from yourself as the person listening to it so you can give it a good hearing.

Second, try to get people to be specific in both their comments and the suggestions they have as to how the situation can be improved.

Third, if possible, get the person complaining to become involved in the solution. For instance, if one person complains about another, ask them if they have approached the person whom they are complaining about. Usually they haven't, so I encourage that they do this, thus having them face the issue instead of dumping it on me. Others try to put me in the middle by telling me things with the proviso that I will not tell the other person they said anything. In most cases I say to them, "I'm sure you wouldn't want to put me in the middle, so if you are going to tell me something, you'll have to stand behind it." Still others are quick to complain and suggest actions but don't see the implications of their proposed moves. For instance, in an elementary school, one teacher might ask for a different grade to teach. In such a instance I would ask the person what he or she would want me to do with the teacher in that position already or how to deal with the others who might also have their eyes on it.

Fourth, no matter how healthy and effective we are in dealing with anger, the residue can build up. Leaders, because of their constant visibility, are bound to incur others' anger either rightly or due to some miscommunication and/or another person's undue sensitivity or expectations. When such a build-up occurs, I do three things: (1) I tease and laugh at myself to diffuse the strain I've put myself under by trying to meet everyone's expectations; (2) I maintain a low profile for a bit and surround myself with sympathetic, supportive people—I don't seek out empathic, problem solvers at this point but people who will say "Oh, you poor sock, how could so-and-so treat you so horribly especially since you're such an angel and you haven't made a mistake since 1949"; and (3) I eventually get people to problem solve with me to break down the complaints and analyze the anger so I can develop strategies to deal with them honestly and effectively.

Failures, small and large, whether we are directly responsible for them or not, are part and parcel of life. The more we worry about them and what people think, the more we will be pulled down.

When people complain and we can see that in our efforts to deal directly with life we have failed, I think we can take a page from the life of Christ, who had to deal with what the world would have viewed as failures in his mission. As John Navone, SJ, aptly notes: "The endurance of failure in any of its many forms is a requisite for salvation; hence, authentic Christian discipleship is an education for failure." Thus, anger and negative criticism of us aren't of themselves very important, but doing everything in our power to learn from them and live through them with perspective and belief in God's love of us are important.

Facing Suppressed Doubt

Belief and doubt have long been discussed as elements of faith in God. Yet, ironically, little has been said about one of the real causes of spiritual paralysis: suppressed doubt.

On the one hand, we have seen the results of trust in the Lord and we can almost hear Christ's words resound: "Your faith has saved you." Likewise, in the Acts of the Apostles we can practically feel the deep trust of the people who believed in Christ's healing presence through Peter: "They all used to meet by common consent in the Portico of Solomon. No one dared to join them, but the people were loud in their praise and the numbers of men and women who came to believe in the Lord increased steadily. So many signs and wonders were worked among the people at the hands of the apostles that the sick were even taken out into the streets and laid on beds and sleeping mats in the hope that at least the shadow of Peter might fall across some of them as he went past" (5:12-16).

In contrast to this, the loud doubting of Thomas who refused to believe unless he personally experienced the presence of the risen Christ leads to the easily recalled statement by Jesus: "Happy are those who have not seen and yet believed" (Jn. 20:29). However, there is another group who neither firmly believe nor loudly doubt. These people, I believe, are very large in number and are quite well represented among those who proclaim themselves as being "religious people." They doubt but are so troubled by it that they have unconsciously or consciously pushed their uncertainty out of their awareness.

The problem is that even though they may not be conscious of it, the doubt still retains a force albeit without there being a clear awareness. Signs of this are possible to note and include: a failure to give first priority to daily prayer (if we believe in God, our relationship with God should be our most important activity during the day; all other prayerful activities would flow from this); our compartmentalization of God to a certain time of day or week without seeing the Spirit's presence in everything; our reliance on doing good rather than being good because of a failure to have hope in God's action in the world; and anxiety over the evil we see in the world today (as if it was proof that God and God's power are but myths).

Given this prevalence of suppressed doubt and the potential harm such avoided and denied doubt can cause even among those who proclaim a desire to be believers, what can be done? Well, I think we need to look at doubt as natural and part of the process of believing. In Thomas Merton's words: "You can't have faith without doubt. Give up the business of suppressing doubt."

In the words of the poet Rainer Maria Rilke: "Be patient toward all that is unsolved in your heart and try to love the questions themselves like locked rooms and like books that are written in a foreign language. Do not now seek the answers, which cannot be given you because you would not be able to live them. And the point is, to live everything. Live the questions now. Perhaps you will then gradually, without noticing it, live along some distant day into the answer."

This is good advice. Doubt and question will always exist. Our choice is to look for God and ask for greater faith amidst the doubt rather than to avoid it or ignore it in our lives. Prayer is a good place to begin because this is the place that each person in a unique way searches for God and screams out for greater faith, greater love, and a deeper sense of courage to commit our lives to living the Gospel at each moment rather than thinking about it only several times each week.

Doubt also assures us that we are not in control and that the very presence of it calls us to be dependent upon God. In commenting on Matt. 14:22-32, William Hulme notes the following: "After a time the disciples believed they saw Jesus coming toward them walking on the water. . . Impulsive by nature, Peter tried to find out. 'Lord, if it is you, bid me come to you on the water'. Jesus told him to come. Peter got out of the boat to do so. Then the Gospel writer says, But when he saw the wind, he was afraid and beginning to sink he cried out, 'Lord, save me'. . . (The implication is that had Peter kept his eyes on Jesus the story might have been different. But Peter deserves credit for knowing what to do when he was sinking—he cried out for help: 'Lord, save me'.) Jesus immediately reached out his hand and caught him."

Living faith and lively doubt go hand in hand. It is in embracing both that we can live not with the false expectation that our doubts will totally disappear, but with the real hope that the doubts, when faced with prayer instead of panic, will lead to a more mature faith and a more creatively lived life.

113

Selected References and Bibliography

Augsburger, David, *Anger And Assertiveness In Pastoral Care*, Fortress Press, Philadelphia, 1979.

Bloom, Anthony, *Beginning To Pray*, Paulist Press, Mahwah, NJ, 1982.

Burns, David, *Feeling Good: The New Mood Therapy*, New American Library, New York, 1981.

Catoir, John, *Enjoy The Lord*, Arena Lettres, Waldwick, NJ, 1979.

Cousins, Norman, *Anatomy Of An Illness*, Norton, New York, 1980.

Delfieux, Pierre-Marie, *The Jerusalem Community Rule Of Life*, Paulist Press, Mahwah, NJ, 1985.

deMello, A. *One Minute Wisdom*, Doubleday Publishing Co., New York, 1986.

Faricy, Robert, SJ, and Wicks, Robert, *Contemplating Jesus*, Paulist Press, Mahwah, NJ, 1986.

Fenhagen, J., *Invitation To Holiness*, Harper & Row Publishers, Inc., San Francisco, 1985.

Foster, Richard, *Celebration Of Discipline: Paths To Spiritual Growth*, Harper & Row Publishers, New York, 1978.

Gonzales-Balado, Jose L. and Playfoot, Janet, (Eds.) *My Life For The Poor: The Story Of Mother Theresa In Her Own Words*, Harper & Row Publishers, Inc., San Francisco, 1985.

Hauser, Richard, *In His Spirit*, Paulist Press, Mahwah, NJ, 1982.

Holmes, Urban, III, *Spirituality For Ministry*, Harper & Row Publishers, New York, 1982.

Johnston, William, SJ, *Christian Mysticism Today*, Harper & Row Publishers, New York, 1984.

Kushner, Harold S., *When Bad Things Happen To Good People*, Schocken Books, New York, 1981.

Leech, Kenneth, *True Prayer: An Invitation To Christian Spirituality*, Harper & Row Publishers, New York, 1981.

Lewis, C.S., *Surprised By Joy*, Harcourt, Brace, New York, 1955.

Merton, Thomas, *New Seeds Of Contemplation*, New York: New Directions, 1961.

Navone, John, SJ, *A Theology Of Failure*, Paulist Press, Mahwah, NJ, 1974.

Nouwen, Henri, *Making All Things New: An Invitation To Life In The Spirit*, Harper & Row Publishers, New York, 1981.

Nouwen, Henri, *Reaching Out*, Doubleday Publishing Co., New York, 1975.

Nouwen, Henri, *The Living Reminder: Service And Prayer In Memory Of Jesus Christ*, Winston Press, Minneapolis, MN, 1981.

Nouwen, Henri, *Way Of The Heart*, Ballantine Books, New York, 1983.

Palmer, Parker, "The Spiritual Life: Apocalypse Now," in Edwards, Tilden, (Ed.) *Living With The Apocalypse*, Harper & Row, Publishers, 1984.

Steindl-Rast, David, *Gratefulness, The Heart Of Prayer: An Approach To Life In Fullness*, Paulist Press, Mahwah, NJ, 1984.

Underwood, Ralph, *Empathy And Confrontation In Pastoral Care*, Westminster, Philadelphia, 1985.

Whitehead, James, "An Asceticism of Time," *Review For Religious*, 39, 1980, p. 3.

Wicks, Robert J., *Availability . . . The Problem And The Gift*, Paulist Press, Mahwah, NJ, 1986.

Wicks, Robert J., *Christian Introspection: Self-Ministry Through Self-Understanding*, Crossroad Publishing Co., New York, 1983.

Wicks, Robert J., *Helping Others: Ways Of Listening, Sharing, Counseling*, Gardner Press, New York, 1982.

Wicks, Robert
Caring for self - Caring
for others